FEB 1 7 2003

MW01278179

LEARNING THE 3 Rs THROUGH ACTIVE PLAY

LEARNING THE 3 Rs THROUGH ACTIVE PLAY

JAMES H. HUMPHREY

Nova Science Publishers, Inc.
New York

Senior Editors: Susan Boriotti and Donna Dennis
Coordinating Editor: Tatiana Shohov
Office Manager: Annette Hellinger
Graphics: Wanda Serrano
Editorial Production: Jennifer Vogt, Matthew Kozlowski, Jonathan Rose
and Maya Columbus
Circulation: Ave Maria Gonzalez, Vera Popovic, Luis Aviles, Melissa Diaz,
Vladimir Klestov and Jeannie Pappas
Communications and Acquisitions: Serge P. Shohov
Marketing: Cathy DeGregory

Library of Congress Cataloging-in-Publication Data
Available Upon Request

ISBN: 1-59033-070-6.

Copyright © 2002 by Snova Books, An Imprint of
Nova Science Publishers, Inc.
400 Oser Ave, Suite 1600
Hauppauge, New York 11788-3619
Tele. 631-231-7269   Fax 631-231-8175
e-mail: Novascience@earthlink.net
Web Site: http://www.novapublishers.com

Printed in the United States of America

You can do anything with children
if you only play with them.

Prince Otto von Bismarck
(1805 – 1898)

CONTENTS

ABOUT THE AUTHOR

James H. Humphrey has been acclaimed for demonstrating experimentally what has been claimed by educational philosophers for centuries, namely, that children tend to learn more readily when learning is associated with meaningful physical activity in the form of active play. Over the years he has authored or co-authored more than 50 books and edited more than 40 others. Dr. Humphrey has received numerous educational honors and awards and his program of active play learning has been featured in a Voice of American broadcast and distributed to its 35 language centers.

INTRODUCTION

In the early days of American education the original 3Rs were considered to be reading, 'riting, and religion. However, later, when arithmetic was introduced into the school program, it replaced religion as the third R. Incidentally, the subject area of arithmetic was changed to elementary school mathematics several decades ago. Nonetheless, we still tend to think of the 3Rs as reading, 'riting, and 'rithmetic, and they are now traditionally referred to as the *basics*.

This book has been prepared for adults – parents, teachers, counselors, and others – and its purpose is to help them help children learn in a pleasurable and enjoyable way. Generally speaking, the book has two important functions. First, it can be used by parents or other adults to help preschoolers get ready for school, and second, adults should find in valuable as a means of helping children after they enter school.

School officials, would like to get adults, particularly parents, more involved in the education of their children. Moreover, many parents themselves want to help their children cope with schoolwork. However, most are at a loss to know where to begin and how to proceed. The material presented in this book should go a long way in helping to meet this need because it provides information on how to assist children in learning through the enjoyable process of active play.

One of the interesting features about the approach recommended in this book in that it not only gives adults an opportunity to help children with the basic 3Rs, but at the same time it makes use of a *basic* need of children –

active play! Through this approach children can learn and improve upon the basic skills in a manner that is enjoyable to both the adult and the child.

It appears appropriate at this point to give the reader a general idea of the content of the book. There are two major reasons for this. First, the reader can get a quick idea of the information contained in the book, and second, it should make for greater ease in reading the individual chapters.

Chapter 1 takes into account the two important aspects of development and learning and one of its features is a discussion of some principles of learning as they apply to active play.

In Chapter 2 different types of learners are identified, including slow-learners, children with learning disabilities, and gifted children.

The third chapter identifies and describes such forms of active play as active games, rhythmic play activities, and stunt play.

In Chapter 4 attention is directed to the subject of *why* children can learn through active play. Many people associate learning only with work and can hardly conceive of how learning can take place through play. It is mainly for this reason that I provide a discussion of the basic theory underlying the active play way of learning. Included is an account of why the active play learning medium is closely related to how children develop, along with a discussion of such factors as motivation, fun and emotional release, and the muscle sense aspect of the active play learning medium.

Since some readers may have had little or no experience in teaching, Chapter 5 goes into some detail about presenting active play learning experiences. Particular attention is devoted to the various phases to the teaching-learning situation as it applies to active play.

Chapter 6 is concerned with ways to improve upon ability to learn through active play. A number of factors that can interfere with a child's ability to learn are identified and discussed, along with how a deficiency in any of these can detract from learning. There is also an account of how the adult can tell if there is such a deficiency, and active play experiences are recommended to help improve upon it.

In Chapters 7-10 there is an overview of the reading process. Detailed information is provided to show how the adult can help the child learn to read through active play. Also discussed are ways to help children to improve their reading ability once they have started to school. This discussion includes how to determine a child's readiness to read, how to improve upon reading skills, and how to improve upon comprehension through this medium. Another interesting feature is the APAV technique to help children learn to read. This procedure should be a welcome one for those adults who like to spend time reading to children.

Chapters 11-14 interpret the meaning of various mathematics programs over the years. Consideration is given to how adults can help the child through active play with such concepts as numeration systems, operations of arithmetic (addition—subtraction—multiplication—division), geometric figures, linear and liquid measurements, telling time, and coin recognition.

The final chapter is concerned with writing readiness and writing problems. The meaning of manuscript and cursive writing is explained along with how the adult can help the child with these. There is a discussion of how active play experiences can be put into writing along with an explanation of how children can learn to write through active play.

Concluding this introduction to the book, I will make some suggestions for its use. The following list of recommendations is suggestive only, because each individual reader will eventually make his or her own decision as to how best use of the book can be obtained. The guidelines submitted here should be viewed with this idea in mind.

Skim through the entire book before attempting to make application of the material that it contains. This should be helpful in providing the reader with an overall understanding of learning through active play.

There are numerous ways to use many of the play activities contained in the book. In many instances the adult can use a one-to-one relationship with the child. In situations where more than two participants are involved, other family members can engage in the activities. The child can be the *principle* player under these conditions. Also, groups of adults may want to cooperate in a kind of active play learning neighborhood undertaking.

Be sure that you know the activity thoroughly before you attempt to teach it to the child. If any material or equipment is necessary it should be readily available.

Make sure the child is having fun in the performance of the activity. If you recognize that it is ceasing to be fun, you can stop and perhaps change to another activity.

Be alert to recognize fatigue symptoms in the child. Regardless of how exciting a learning activity may be, little or no learning is likely to take place when a child has become fatigued.

The time of day to conduct the activities is very important. For preschool children, about midmorning is a good time. Adults may wish to set aside a certain time each day for these activities. On the other hand, it can be very effective when an experience develops in a more or less spontaneous manner. With school age children each individual adult will no doubt find the most suitable time for the activities. Ordinarily, it is not considered a good practice to engage in anything related to school immediately when he or she returns home from school.

Give the child praise for performance. Such positive reinforcement is likely to inspire him or her to want to continue with the experience.

Try to structure the active play learning experience in such a way as to allow the child to succeed. Too many children have too many failures early in life. Thus, it is most important that children have a feeling of success so as to build confidence in themselves.

The suggestions set forth consist of only a few of the possibilities for use of the book. Each individual reader will find numerous other ways to apply the material.

A book is seldom the sole product of the author. Admittedly, the author does most of the things concerned with actually putting a book together, from the germ of the idea to eventually getting it published. However, it is almost always true that many individuals participate, at least indirectly, in some way before a book is finally completed. This volume is no exception. To acknowledge everyone personally would be practically impossible. Therefore, I would like to acknowledge collectively the hundreds of parents, teachers, and children who participated so willingly in my experiments with the active play experiences, and thus made this final volume possible.

Chapter 1

DEVELOPMENT AND LEARNING

Recognizing a child's mannerisms and his or her likes and dislikes does not necessarily mean that an adult has a full understanding of child development and learning. Even those professional workers who spend their time studying about children are not always in complete agreement with regard to the complex nature of child development. The major purpose of this initial chapter is to present general information on this subject. This means that the discussion will be concerned with the so-called "average" child. It should be remembered that averages tend to be arrived at mathematically and that a child develops at his or her own rate. It is quite likely that a child may be above average in some characteristics and below average in others. It is important that adults realize this; thus, the materials in this chapter should be considered with this idea in mind.

MEANING OF TERMS

To avoid confusion, it seems appropriate to convey to the reader the meaning of certain terms used in this chapter. The two major terms that we are concerned with are *development* and *learning*.

Development is concerned with changes in the child's ability to function at an increasingly higher level. For example, a stage of development in the infant is from creeping to crawling. This is later followed by the developmental stage of walking when the child moves to an upright position and begins to propel himself over the surface area by putting one foot in from in front of the other.

Most definitions of *learning* are characterized by the idea that it involves some sort of change in the individual. This means that when an individual has learned, his or her behavior is modified in one or more ways. Thus, a good standard for learning would be that after having had an experience one could behave in a way in which he or she could not have behaved before he had the experience. In this general connection, many learning theorists suggest that it is not possible to *see* learning. However, behavior can be seen, and when a change in behavior has occurred, then it is possible to infer that change and learning have occurred. This concept is depicted in the following diagram.

Learning Can Be Inferred by a Change in Behavior

Child behaves → Child is in a learning → Child behaves in a way that
in a given way   situation   is different from before he
                                           was in the learning situation

The essential difference between development and learning is that development deals with general abilities while learning is concerned with specific behaviors. When it is considered that development of children brings about needs, and that these needs must be met satisfactorily, the importance of an understanding of development is readily seen. When an understanding of the various aspects of development is accomplished, adults are then in a better position to provide improved procedures for meeting the needs of children. This implies that we might be guided by what could be called a *developmental philosophy* if we are to meet with any degree of success in our dealings with children.

TOTAL PERSONALITY DEVELOPMENT

Total development is the fundamental purpose of the education of children. All attempts at such education should take into account a combination of *physical, social, emotional* and *intellectual* aspects of human behavior. Thus, these are the forms of development that I will consider in the discussion here. Of course, there are other forms of development, but they can be subclassified under one of these areas. For instance, *motor development,* which can be described as progressive change in motor performance, is considered as a part of the broader aspect of *physical development*. In addition, *moral development*, which is concerned with the capacity of the individual to distinguish between standards of right and wrong, could be considered a dimension of the broad aspect of *social development*. This is to say that moral development involving achievement in the ability to determine right from wrong is influential in the individual's social behavior.

A great deal of clinical and experimental evidence indicates that a human being must be considered as a *whole* and not a collection of parts. For purposes here I prefer to use the term *total personality* in referring to the child as a unified individual or total being. Perhaps a more common term is *whole child*. However, the term total personality is commonly used in the field of psychology, and it is being increasingly used in the field of education. Moreover, considering it from a point of view of man existing as a person, it is interesting to note that "existence as a person" is one rather common definition of personality.

The total personality consists of the sum of all the physical, social, emotional, and intellectual aspects of any individual; that is, the major forms of development previously identified. The total personality is *one thing* comprising these various aspects. All of these components are highly interrelated and interdependent. All are of importance to the balance and health of the personality because only in terms of the health of each can the personality as a whole maintain a completely healthful state. The condition of any one aspect affects each other aspect to a degree and thus the personality as a whole.

When a nervous child stutters or becomes nauseated, a mental state is not necessarily causing a physical symptom. On the contrary, a pressure imposed upon the organism causes a series of reactions that include thought, verbalization, digestive processes, and muscular function. It is not that the mind causes the body to be upset; the total organism is upset by a situation and reflects its upset in several ways, including disturbance in thought, feeling, and bodily processes. The whole individual responds in interaction with the social and physical environment, and as the individual is affected by the environment, he or she, in turn, has an effect upon it.

However, because of long tradition during which physical development *or* intellectual development, rather than physical development *and* intellectual development has been glorified, we are often still accustomed to dividing the two in our thinking.

Traditional attitudes that separate the mind and body tend to lead to unbalanced development of the child with respect to mind and body and/or social adjustment. What is more important is that we fail to use the strengths of one to serve the needs of the other.

The foregoing statements have attempted to point out rather forcefully the idea that the identified components of the total personality comprise the unified individual That each of these aspects might well be considered separately should also be taken into account. As such, each aspect should warrant a separate discussion. This appears extremely important if one is to understand fully the place of each aspect as an integral part of the total personality. The following discussions of the physical, social, emotional, and intellectual aspects of personality should be viewed in this general frame of reference.

The Physical Aspect of Personality

One point of departure in discussing the physical aspect of personality could be to state that "everybody has a body." Some are short, some are tall, some are lean, and some are fat. Children come in different sizes, but all of them have a certain innate capacity that is influenced by the environment.

It might be said of the child that he *is* his body. It is something he can see. It is his base of operation – or what might be termed the *physical base*. The other components of the total personality – social, emotional, and intellectual – are somewhat vague as far as the child is concerned. Although these are manifested in various ways, children do not always see them as they do the physical aspect. Consequently, it becomes all important that a child be helped early in life to gain control over the physical aspect, or what is known as basic body control The ability to do this will vary from one child to another. It will depend upon the status of *physical fitness* of the child. The broad area of physical fitness can be broken down into certain components, and it is important that individuals achieve to the best of their natural ability as far as these components are concerned. There is not complete agreement as far as identification of the components of physical fitness are concerned. However, the President's Council on Physical Fitness and Sports considers these components to consist of the following:

1. Muscular strength (the contraction power of the muscles).
2. Muscular endurance (ability of the muscles to perform work).
3. Circulatory-respiratory endurance (moderate contractions of large muscle groups for relatively long periods of time).
4. Muscular power (ability to release maximum muscular force in the shortest time).
5. Agility (speed in changing direction, or body position).
6. Speed (rapidity with which successive movements of the same kind can be performed).
7. Flexibility (range of movement in a joint or a sequence of joints).
8. Balance (ability to maintain position and equilibrium).
9. Coordination (working together of the muscles in the performance of a specific task).

The components of physical fitness and, thus, the physical aspect of personality can be measured by precise instruments, such as measurements of muscular strength. Moreover, we can tell how tall a child is or how heavy he or she is at any stage of development. In addition, medically trained personnel can derive other accurate information with assessments of blood pressure, blood counts and urinalysis.

The Social Aspect of Personality

Human beings are social beings. They work together for the benefit of society. They have fought together in time of national emergencies to preserve the kind of society they believe in, and they play together. While all this may be true, the social aspect of personality still is quite vague and confusing particularly as far as children are concerned.

It was a relatively easy matter to identify certain components of physical fitness such as strength and endurance. However, this does not necessarily hold true for components of social fitness. The components for physical fitness are the same for children as for adults. On the other hand, the components of social fitness for children may be different from the components of social fitness for adults. By some adult standards children might be considered as social misfits because certain behavior of children might not be socially acceptable to some adults.

To the dismay of some adults, young children are uninhibited as far as the social aspect of personality is concerned. In this regard, we need to be concerned with social maturity as it pertains to the growing and ever-changing child. We need to give consideration to certain characteristics of social maturity and how they are dealt with at the different stages of child development.

Perhaps adults need to ask themselves such questions as: Am I helping the child to become self-reliant by giving him or her independence at the proper time? Am I helping him or her to be outgoing and interested in others as well as himself or herself? Am I helping the child to know how to satisfy his or her own needs in a socially desirable way?

The Emotional Aspect of Personality

For many years, emotion has been a difficult concept to define; in addition, there have been many changing ideas and theories as far as the study of emotion is concerned.

Obviously, it is not the purpose of a book of this nature to attempt to go into any great depth on a subject that has been one of the most intricate undertakings of psychology for many years. A few general statements, however, do seem to be in order if we are to understand more clearly this aspect of personality.

Emotion is a response a person makes to a stimulus for which he or she is not adequately prepared. For example, if a child is confronted with a situation and does not have a satisfactory response, the emotional pattern of fear may result. If one finds him or herself in a position where desires are frustrated, the emotional pattern of anger may occur. It is interesting to note that *reading* and *mathematics* are school subject areas that are loaded with emotion and frustration for many children. In fact, one of the levels of reading recognized by reading specialists is called the "frustration level" In behavioral observation terms this can be described as the level at which children evidence distracting tension, excessive or erratic body movements, nervousness and distractibility. This frustration level is said to be a sign of emotional tension or stress with breakdowns in fluency and a significant increase in reading errors. (One of the important aspects of the active play approach is that the child is relieved of this emotional stress in this pleasurable approach to reading).

The area of mathematics is so emotionally charged that there is now an area of study known as *Math Anxiety* that is receiving increasing attention.

There appear to be what could be called "math anxious" and "math avoiding" people who tend not to trust their problem-solving abilities and who experience a high level of stress when asked to use them. Even though theses people are not necessarily "mathematically ignorant," they tend to feel that they are, simply because they cannot focus on the problem at hand or because they are unable to remember the appropriate formula. Thus, feelings of frustration and incompetence are likely to make them reluctant to deal with mathematics in their daily lives. It is believed that at the root of this self-doubt is a fear of making mistakes and appearing stupid in front of others.

One of the strongest memories of math-anxious adults is the feeling of humiliation when being called upon to perform in front of the class. The child may be asked to go to the chalkboard and struggle over a problem until the solution is found. If an error is made the child may be prodded to locate and correct it. In this kind of stressful situation it is not surprising that the child is likely to experience "math block," which adds to the sense of humiliation and failure. This should not be interpreted to mean that the chalkboard should not be used creatively to demonstrate problem-solving abilities. A child who successfully performs a mathematical task in front of classmates can have the enjoyable experience of instructing others. Also the rest of the class can gain useful information from watching how another solves a problem. When using chalkboard practice, however, it is important to remember that children profit from demonstrating their competence and not their weaknesses. (As in the case of reading, one of the important aspects of the active play approach is that the child is relieved of emotional stress in this pleasurable approach to learning about mathematics.)

Emotions might be classified in two different ways – those that are *pleasant* and those that are *unpleasant.* For example, *joy* could be considered as a pleasant emotional experience while *fear* would be an unpleasant one. It is interesting that a good proportion of the literature is devoted to emotions that are unpleasant. It has been found that in psychology books much more space is given to such emotional patterns as fear and anger than to such pleasant emotions as joy and contentment.

Generally speaking, the pleasantness or unpleasantness of an emotion seems to be determined by its strength or intensity, by the nature of the situation arousing it, and by the way an individual perceives or interprets the situation. As far as children are concerned, their emotions tend to be more intense than those of adults. If an adult is not aware of this aspect of child behavior, he or she will not likely understand why a child may react rather violently to a situation that to the adult seems somewhat insignificant. It should also be taken into account that different children will react differently to the same type of situation. For example, something that might anger one child might have a rather passive influence on another. In this regard, it is interesting to observe the effect that winning or losing has on certain children.

The Intellectual Aspect of Personality

The word intelligence is derived from the Latin word *intellectus*, which literally means the "power of knowing." Intelligence has been described in many ways. One general description of it is the "capacity to learn or understand."

Individuals possess varying degrees of intelligence, and most people fall within a range of what is called "normal" intelligence. In dealing with this aspect of personality attention should be given to what might be considered some components of intellectual fitness. However, this is difficult to do. Because of the somewhat vague nature of intelligence, it is practically impossible to identify specific components of it. Thus, we need to view intellectual fitness in a somewhat different manner.

For purposes of this discussion I will consider intellectual fitness from two difference, but closely related points of view: first, from a standpoint of intellectual needs and second, from a standpoint of how certain things influence intelligence. It might be said that if a child's intellectual needs are being met then perhaps we could also say that he or she is intellectually fit. From the second point of view, if we know how certain things influence intelligence then we might understand better how to contribute to intellectual fitness by improving upon these factors.

There appears to be some rather general agreement with regard to the intellectual needs of children. Among others, these include: (1) a need to challenging experiences at the child's level of ability, (2) a need for intellectually successful and satisfying experiences, (3) a need for the opportunity to solve problems, and (4) a need for the opportunity to participate in creative experiences instead of always having to conform.

Some of the factors that tend to influence intelligence are (1) health and physical condition, (2) emotional disturbance, and (3) certain social and economic factors.

When adults have a realization of intellectual needs and factors influencing intelligence, perhaps then, and only then, can they deal satisfactorily with children in helping them in their intellectual pursuits.

It was mentioned that an important intellectual need for children is the opportunity to participate in creative experiences. This need is singled out for special attention because the opportunities for creative experiences are perhaps more evident in active play situations than in almost any other single aspect of the child's life.

DEVELOPMENTAL CHARACTERISTICS OF CHILDREN

As the child progresses through various stages of development certain distinguishing characteristics can be identified which furnish implications for effective teaching and learning.

The range of age levels from 5 through 7 usually includes children from kindergarten through Grade 2. During this period the child begins formal education. In our culture the child leaves the home and family constellation for a part of the day to take his or her place in a classroom of children approximately the same chronological age. Not only is the child taking an important step toward becoming increasingly more independent and self-reliant, but he or she moves from being a highly self-centered, egotistical individual to becoming a more socialized group member.

This stage is characterized by a certain lack of motor coordination, because the small muscles of the hands and fingers are not as well developed as the large muscles of the arms and legs. Thus, as he or she starts formal education there is a need to use large crayons or pencils as one means of expression. The urge to action is expressed through movement and noise. Children at these age levels thrive on vigorous activity. They develop as they climb, run, jump, hop, skip, or keep time to music. An important physical aspect at this level is that the eyeball is increasing in size and the eye muscles are developing. This factor is an important determinant in the child's readiness to see and read small print, and thus involves a sequence from large print to charts to primer type in preprimers and primers.

Even though there is a relatively short attention span, he or she is extremely curious about the environment. At this stage the adult capitalizes upon the child's urge to learn by providing opportunities for him or her to gain information from firsthand experiences through the use of the senses. The child sees, hears, smells, feels, tastes and of course plays in order to learn.

The age range of 8 and 9 years is the period, which usually marks the time, spent in third and fourth grades. The child now has a wider range of interest and longer attention span. While strongly individualistic, he or she is working from a position in a group. Organized games afford opportunities for developing and practicing skills in good leadership and followership, as well as body control, strength and endurance. Small muscles are developing, manipulative skills are increasing, and muscular coordination is improving. The eyes have developed so that some children can, and do, read more widely. They are capable of getting information from books and are beginning to learn through vicarious experience. However, experiments carry an impact for learning at this age by capitalizing upon the child's curiosity as he or she tests or proves a hypothesis. This is the stage in development when skills of communication (listening, speaking, reading, and writing) and the number system are needed to deal with situations in and out of school.

At the age range of 10 through 12 most children complete the fifth and sixth grades. This is a period of transition for most, as they go from childhood into the preadolescent period of their development. They may show concern over bodily changes, and are sometimes self-conscious about appearance. At this range of age levels children tend to differ widely in physical maturation and in emotional stability. Greater deviations in growth and development can be noticed within the sex groups than between them. Rate of physical growth can be rapid, sometimes showing itself in poor posture and restlessness. Some of the more highly organized games such as softball, modified soccer, and the like, help to furnish the keen and wholesome competition desired by these children. It is essential that an adult recognize that at this level prestige among peers can be more important than adult approval. During this period the child is ready for a higher level of intellectual skills, involving reasoning, discerning fact from opinion, noting cause-and-effect relationships, drawing conclusions, and using various references to locate and compare the validity of information. Children are beginning to show proficiency in expressing themselves through oral and written communication.

Thus, during the years between kindergarten and the completion of Grade 6, the child develops (1) socially, from a self-centered individual to a participating member of a group, (2) emotionally, from a state manifesting temper tantrums to a higher degree of self-control, (3) physically, from childhood to the brink of adolescence and (4) intellectually, from learning from firsthand experiences to learning from technical and specialized resources.

If the child is to be educated as a growing organism, aspects of development need the utmost consideration of adults in planning and guiding learning activities, which will be most profitable for the child at his or her particular stage of development.

THE NATURE OF LEARNING

The learning process is complicated and complex, and the task of explaining it has occupied the attention of psychologists for many years. In recent years this effort has been intensified and more about learning is being discovered almost daily. It is not my intent to try to go into depth on anything as complicated as the learning process. On the other hand, it will be my purpose to make some general statements about it as well as to consider certain conditions under which learning is most likely to take place. The reason for this is that, although it is not definitely known what happens when learning takes place, a great deal is known about the conditions under which it can take place most effectively.

The word *learning* is used in many connections. We speak of learning how to walk, how to speak, how to make a living, and how to feel about various things such as failing, aggressiveness, going to school, and so forth. As mentioned, whatever kind of learning one is concerned with, specialists seem to agree that it involves some kind of change in behavior. Obviously, the concern here is with changes in behavior that are brought about by child-adult relationships with particular reference to active play.

Just what does change in behavior mean? This is an extremely important question because it suggests that the child proceeds promptly to behave in a certain way as a result of a child-adult interaction in an active play situation. The word *behavior* can refer to improved understandings as reflected verbally and/or in writing. Thus, even though a child cannot always change his or her behavior in terms of practical performance and actually *do* what he or she has learned, the child can reflect greater understanding in written or spoken behavior. Moreover, he or she can reflect it in contrived classroom situations where he or she is able to act as though the improved understandings were being carried into actual situations. Unfortunately, some teachers may not worry too much about changes in a child's behavior beyond what can be accomplished on a written test.

SOME PRINCIPLES OF LEARNING APPLIED TO ACTIVE PLAY

There are various facts about the nature of human beings of which modern educators are more aware than educators of the past. Essentially, these facts involve some of the fundamental aspects of the learning process, which all good teaching should take into account. Older ideas of teaching methods were based on the notion that the teacher was the sole authority in terms of what was best for children, and that children were expected to learn regardless of the conditions surrounding the learning situation. For the most part, modern teaching replaces the older concept with methods that are based on certain beliefs of educational psychology. Outgrowths of these beliefs emerge in the form of *principles of learning*. The following principles should provide important guidelines for adults for arranging learning experiences for children and they suggest how desirable learning can take place when the principles are satisfactorily applied to learning through active play.

1. *The child's own purposeful goals should guide learning activities.* For a desirable learning situation to prevail, adults should consider certain features about purposeful goals that guide learning activities. Of utmost importance is that the goal must seem worthwhile to the child. This will involve such factors as interest, attention, and motivation. Fortunately, in the recommended activities in this book involving learning the 3Rs through active play, interest, attention, and motivation are "built-in" qualities. Thus, the adult does not necessarily need to "arouse" the child with various kinds of extrinsic motivating devices.

2. *The child should be given sufficient freedom to create his or her own responses in the situation faced.* This principle indicates that *problem*

solving is a very important way of human learning and that the child will learn mainly only through experience, either direct or indirect. This implies that an adult should provide every opportunity for the child to use judgement in the various situations that arise in the active play experience.

3. *The child agrees to and acts upon the learnings that he or she considers of most value.* Children accept as most valuable those things, which are of greatest interest to them. This principle implies, in part, that there should be a satisfactory balance between *needs* and *interests* of children in their active play experiences. Although it is of extreme importance to consider the needs of children in developing experiences, an adult should keep in mind that their interest is needed if the most desirable learning is to take place.

4. *The child should be given the opportunity to share cooperatively in learning experiences with others under the guidance but not the control of the adult.* This principle is concerned with those active play experiences that involve several players. The point that should be emphasized here is that although learning is an individual matter, it can take place well in a group. This is to say that children learn individually but that socialization should be retained. This can be achieved even if there are only two members participating, the adult and the child.

5. *The adult should act as a guide who understands the child as a growing organism.* This principle indicates that the adult should consider learning as an evolving process and not just as an instant behavior. If an adult is to regard his or her efforts in terms of guidance and direction of behavior that results in learning, wisdom must be displayed as to when to "step in and teach and when to step aside and watch for further opportunities to guide and direct behavior." The application of this principle precludes an approach that is adult dominated. In this regard the adult could be guided by the old saying that "children should learn by monkeying and not by aping."

It is quite likely that adults will have good success in using the active play experiences recommended in this book if they to apply the above principles. The main reason for this is that their efforts in helping children learn about the 3Rs through active play will be in line with those conditions under which learning takes place most effectively. (Chapter 5 will discuss specifically how to conduct the active play learning experience.)

Chapter 2

IDENTIFYING TYPES OF LEARNERS

The basic principle of *teaching to the individual differences of the learner* has led to the development of many components within the educational system. Programs and services that reflect the needs of those with widely varying abilities are available in most school systems.

SLOW LEARNING CHILDREN

Over the years there has developed a national concern for the problems of children with learning impairment. Direct grants for research and services for these children have enabled government agencies and private foundations to work cooperatively to help the schools do a better job, both in identifying these children and providing more appropriate learning environments for them. The neurologist, the physician, the psychologist, and the researcher in education have contributed new insights into working with these children.

Some of the research in ways children with mental deficits and impairment learn provides the teacher with useful guidelines. Research has been directed not only to the etiology, the nature, and the degree of learning impairment, but also to the educational environment within which learning takes place for children with such impairments.

Identifying the Slow Learner

While there has been agreement that the needs of children with learning impairment must be reflected in appropriate teaching techniques, there is an increasing awareness of the problems of identification. Too many children have been mistaken for slow learners because of their difficulties in mastering such academic skills as mathematics and reading. It is essential, therefore, that there can be a clear understanding of basic differences among children with the *slow learner syndrome*, but whose learning problems may be caused by factors other than subnormal intellectual functioning. With this general frame of reference in mind, the subsequent discussions will focus upon slow learners classified as (1) the child with mental retardation, (2) the child with depressed potential, and (3) the child with a learning disability.

The Child with Mental Retardation

In the literature the broad generic term mentally retarded encompasses all degrees of mental deficit. The designation of the term slow learner has been given to those children who have a mild degree (along a continuum) of subnormal intellectual functioning as measured by intelligence tests. The intelligence quotients of these children fall within the range of 70 or 75 to 90. This child makes average or below average progress in the academic skills, depending where he or she falls along the continuum of mental retardation. The child will probably demonstrate slowness in learning such academic skills as mathematics and reading. He or she will very likely have difficulty in the area of more complex mental processes of defining, analyzing, and comparing. The child tends to be a poor reasoner. However, he or she need not necessarily be equally slow in all aspects of behavior. For instance, the child may be above average in social adaptability or artistic endeavors.

In respect to physical characteristics, personality, and adjustment, slow-learning children are as variable and heterogeneous as children in the average and above-average range of intellectual potential. Attributes often identified with slow learners are laziness, inattention, and short attention span. However, these characteristics are likely to be eliminated when the educational environment is geared to the needs of children and when there is appropriateness, meaningfulness, and purposefulness to the learning activity.

There is some variance in the literature as to whether these children should be identified as mentally retarded. There is general agreement that the slow learner represents a mild degree of subnormal intellectual functioning, whether or not he or she is labeled mentally retarded. Characteristic educational life patterns of those within the broad educational categories of subnormal intelligence can be described as: (1) the slow learner, (2) the educable mentally retarded, (3) the trainable mentally retarded, and (4) the totally dependent mentally retarded. With reference to the slow learner it is suggested that this type of child is not considered mentally retarded because he or she is able to achieve a moderate degree of academic success even though at a lower rate than the average child. He or she is educated in the regular class program to fit the slower learning ability. At the adult level the person is usually self-supporting, independent, and socially adjusted.

In the past several years the dimension of social adaptiveness has gained as an influencing criterion for identification of the mentally retarded. For example, the criterion of social acceptance has been emphasized in terms of the growing reluctance to identify persons as mentally retarded on the basis of intellectual subnormality alone.

Thus, a person who scores 65 on an intelligence test and who at the same time shows ability to adapt to the social demands of the particular environment at home, work, and in the community should not necessarily be considered retarded. Indeed, it is now known that he or she is not generally so considered.

It is apparent, therefore, that the slow learner with whom the teacher may be working in the classroom may have significant intellectual subnormality.

The Child with Depressed Potential

For a good many years it has been recognized that factors other than intellectual subnormality affect achievement in the classroom. Concern in our schools today for the disadvantaged and culturally different children is placing increased emphasis on an understanding of these factors. The groundwork was laid several decades ago when Featherstone[1] considered these factors in his delineation of the limited education achievement of the constitutional slow learner with subnormal intellectual capacity from the functional slow learner. The latter is often mistaken by teachers for a slow learner with limited potential because he or she is having difficulty achieving in the classroom.

The child may be making limited progress in acquiring the academic skills or may be a behavior problem, but his or her limited achievements are caused by numerous other factors that serve to depress an individual's ability to learn. Such factors may be lack of psychological stimulation from limited socioeconomic environment, inadequate hearing and vision, emotional problems in relationships with family and peers, malnutrition or poor general health. It is important to recognize that the situation is not necessarily permanent. Both educational programs and conditions affecting the child's physical, social, emotional and intellectual well being can be improved.

The Child with a Learning Disability

A further compounding of the problem of identification of the slow learner has occurred with studies of children who do not come under the categories of the constitutional or functional slow learner, but whose classroom achievement may be similar. Often the learning-disabled child is called stupid or lazy, or both. The child is neither and such labels can have a negative influence on learning as well as self-concept.

The research identifying learning-disability children indicates that their learning has been impaired in specific areas of verbal and/or nonverbal learning, but their potential for learning is categorized as normal or above. Thus, these learning-disability children fall with the 90 and above IQ range in either the verbal or nonverbal areas. Total IQ is not used as the criterion for determining learning potential inasmuch as adequate intelligence, either verbal or nonverbal, is obscured in cases where the total IQ falls below 90, but in which specific aspects of intelligence fall within the definition of adequate intelligence. The learning-disability child whose IQ falls below the normal range, and where a learning disability is present is considered to have a multiple involvement.

In learning disability children there are deficits in verbal and/or nonverbal learning. There may be impairment of expressive, receptive or integrative functions. There is concern for deficits in the function of input and output, of sensory modalities, and of degree of impairment.

The learning-disability child shows marked differences from the child with limited potential. There are both qualitative and quantitative differences. The learning-disability child has more potential for learning. The means by which he learns may be different. (Chapter 6 goes into detail about improving learning ability through active play.)

While there may be some overlapping in the educational methods used with these three groups identified as slow learners, there obviously must be differentiation in educational goals and approaches for these various groups. Correct identification of the factors causing slowness in learning is essential in teaching with the individual differences among children.

Learning Characteristics of Slow Learners

When considering educational processes that would provide a successful learning experience for children with limited intellectual potential, it is necessary to examine some of their basic characteristics of learning. Slow learners appear to follow the same patterns as those who have more adequate intellectual endowment in terms of the sequences of growth and development. The basic difference is the time schedule at which these children arrive at various levels of development. Theoretically, the child with an IQ of 80 develops intellectually at a rate only four-fifths that of the average child. The rate of development of these children is more closely correlated with their mental age than their chronological age.

Differences have been found in comparisons of the learning process in mathematics and reading of mentally retarded and normal children. However, these differences are not necessarily always attributable to ability to learn, but perhaps in some cases more to the influence of teaching methods. Included among the factors affecting the learning process are the value systems of the individual and his or her own concept of self as a learner. These two factors must be recognized as particularly important. The reason for this is that there are so many negative psychological factors operating within the life space of large percentages of the mentally retarded who can maintain themselves only in a low socioeconomic environment.

GIFTED AND TALENTED CHILDREN

When we get into any kind of labeling in education we have problems, not only with communication with individuals outside a given field but also with workers in the field itself. This seems to be the case with the terms gifted and talented because there is still a fair amount of disagreement among professionals themselves regarding the meaning of these terms.

Definitions of giftedness in the mid 1900s focused on IQ or intellectual ability as the main indicator of giftedness. The gifted individual was viewed as one possessing a high level of intelligence, which, in turn was seen as a fixed and measurable quantity. Correspondingly, the gifted child could be easily defined as a person with an IQ of at or above an established point. (Some current estimates suggest that gifted students with IQs of 130 and above comprise about three percent of the school population.) The fact that this situation is still somewhat widespread today is shown in a study[2] that revealed that dependence upon measures of cognitive ability are the prevailing identification tools used in selecting children for programs for the gifted and/or talented. Although achievement tests appear to have replaced IQ tests as keystone instruments, they reflect an academic posture similar to that of IQ tests and support the intellectual aura characteristic of programs for the gifted/talented historically evident in the 20th century. In other words, they sample extant knowledge or skills – perhaps to a degree even greater than IQ tests. Over 90 percent of the programs identified gifted with achievement tests and almost 75 percent used IQ tests for this purpose. This finding tends to contradict the current popular rhetoric which recommends that behavioral data replace the role of hard-line cognitive test scores as a means of identifying gifted children.

It is interesting to note that the terms gifted and talented are often defined in combination. Traditionally, as mentioned above, giftedness has been associated with extraordinary intellectual ability, and there are many persons who have high levels of intelligence who also display special talent. However, on the contrary, one could have a special talent and at the same time have so-called normal intelligence.

In this general regard, it is interesting to note that the United States Congress in passing legislation authorizing allocations of funds for education of the gifted a good many years ago used a broad definition suggested by a special study on the status of education of the gifted in this country[3]. This study reported that gifted and talented children are those identified by professionally qualified persons who by virtue of outstanding abilities are capable of high performance. These are children who require differentiated educational programs and/or services beyond those normally provided by the regular school program in order to realize their contributions to self and society. Children capable of high performance include those with demonstrated achievement and/or potential ability in any of the following areas, singly or in combination.

1. General intellectual ability.
2. Specific academic aptitude.
3. Creative or productive thinking.
4. Leadership ability.
5. Visual and performing arts.
6. Psychomotor ability.

It was assumed that utilization of these criteria for identification of the gifted and talented would encompass a minimum of three to five percent of the total school population. (Incidentally, it is estimated that only about one-half of the gifted children in this country have been identified as such, and that only about one-third are being served by special school programs.) In any case, the Gifted and Talented Children's Educational Act of 1978 utilized the following description: "Gifted and talented children means children and, where applicable, youth, who are identified at the preschool, elementary, or secondary level as possessing demonstrated potential abilities that give evidence of high performance capability in areas such as intellectual, creative, specific academic, or leadership ability, or in the performing and visual arts, and who by reason thereof, require services or activities not ordinarily provided by the school."

Later, the language used in P. L. 97-35, the Education Consolidation and Improvement Act, passed by Congress in 1981 was: "Gifted and talented children are now referred to as children who give evidence of high performance capability in areas such as intellectual, creative, artistic, leadership capacity, or specified academic fields, and who require services or activities not ordinarily provided by the school in order to fully develop such capabilities."

It should be readily observed that all of the language used in the above descriptions is characterized more by likeness than by difference. Moreover, the above focuses on those more or less positive traits and characteristics of gifted children.

One well-known authority on the subject Virginia Erlich[4], once suggested that besides identifying gifted children by means of known positive traits, adult leaders should reevaluate the child who shows the following negative characteristics that may be clues to unrecognized giftedness.

1. Excessive restlessness or diagnosed hyperactivity.
2. Mischief making, especially if it is associated with a sharp sense of humor.
3. Poor achievement, even though other behavior contradicts this evidence.
4. Leadership as recognized by peers, for example, leading a gang.
5. Withdrawal, indifference, inattention, daydreaming in class.
6. Excessive cutting (skipping school).
7. Unwillingness to do homework.
8. Persistence in pursuing a discussion or topic beyond the teacher's expressed cutoff point.

I hasten to mention that the above should not be interpreted to mean that gifted children are necessarily behavior problems. On the contrary, some research has shown that gifted elementary school students show fewer behavior problems than their non-gifted classmates.

Since intellectual ability still appears to be the primary attribute as far as gifted children are concerned, it seems important to comment further on this. Several years ago representatives of the American Association for Gifted Children[5] suggested that generally the following evidence would indicate special intellectual gifts or talents.

1. Consistently very superior scores on many appropriate standardized tests.
2. Demonstration of advanced skills, imaginative thought, and intense interest and involvement.
3. Judgement of teachers, administrators, supervisors, and specialists in various fields, including the arts, who are familiar with the abilities and potential of the individual and are qualified to evaluate them.

In closing this chapter I want to caution that as most readers are aware, an extremely high IQ does not necessarily guarantee success in the classroom. In my own work[6] as well as that of others in the area of childhood stress it has been demonstrated time and again that children who come from families in stress have difficulty coping with stress themselves. Sometimes this inability to cope has resulted in a child scoring several points lower on an intelligence test than would otherwise be the case. Therefore, it is possible that in those schools where IQ tests are the sole means used for determining placement of children in special programs for the gifted, children with stressful personal and family lives are being placed in programs below their potential. With good stress management for these children a normal child actually may turn out to be gifted.

Another factor to consider is that some children with an extremely high IQ may suffer from certain kinds of learning disabilities that inhibit their ability to develop skills and concepts even at the average level. While this population is estimated at only five to eight percent, these children experience much more trauma than the so-called normal child does when a learning disability is present. As I have mentioned, children with learning disabilities are difficult to identify; that is, with traditional procedures. The "normal" gifted child is frequently overlooked on group administered tests; in fact, it has been indicated that up to 70 percent of gifted children may not be identified if only group tests are used. Gifted children with learning disabilities perform very poorly on these group tests, especially when their deficiency is in the area of visual perception and they cannot read with understanding. It is even more critical that these children be given individually administered tests than the "normal" gifted child is. Not only will individualized tests indicate their high intelligence, but it will also point out the area in which learning disabilities exist, such as perceptual and/or motor.

Finally, another consideration that might be addressed is the person with a below normal IQ who might be gifted, at least in some way. As an extreme example, take the case of the idiot savant. Psychologists have puzzled over the idiot savant for years. Some say that these people have defective abstract reasoning ability and must rely only on concrete thought processes. Others theorize that idiot savants are the product of their families and early environments. (Some readers may perhaps recall the 1988 movie, The Rain Man, in which Dustin Hoffman portrayed the character of an "autistic savant.")

NOTES

[1] Featherstone, W. B., Teaching the slow learner, In Caswell, Hollis L., (Ed.) *Practical Suggestions for Teaching*, 2nd Ed. New York, Teachers College, Columbia University, 1951, No 1, pp. 10-11.

[2] Yarborough, Betty H. and Johnson, Roger A., *Identifying the Gifted: A theory-practice gap*, Gifted Child Quarterly, Summer 1983.

[3] Marland, Sidney P., Jr., *Education of the Gifted and Talented*, Report to the United States Congress by the Commissioner of Education, Washington, DC, U. S. Department of Health, Education and Welfare, 1971.

[4] Ehrlich, Virginia Z., *Gifted Children: A Guide for Parents and Teachers*, Englewood Cliffs, Prentice-Hall, Inc. 1982, p. 164.

[5] Tannenbaum, Abraham J. and Neuman, Elizabeth, *Reaching Out: Advocacy for the Gifted and Talented*, American Association for Gifted Children, Teachers College, Columbia University, New York 1980.

[6] Humphrey, James H., *Helping Children Manage Stress*, Washington, DC, Child and Family Press, 1998.

Chapter 3

FORMS OF ACTIVE PLAY

The difficulty in defining the term play is shown by the fact that most standard dictionaries give almost 60 definitions of the term. Perhaps the reason for this is that the word play is used in so many different ways. This tends to require that authors who write about the subject of play give their own operational definition of it.

My description of active play is any enjoyable interaction with one or more persons and/or natural forces. This description places emphasis on active play as opposed to that, which is more passive in nature. The kind of play I am concerned with is that which involves a total or near total physical response on the part of the child as he or she interacts with others and/or natural forces. When I use the term natural forces I am concerned primarily with the child playing by him or herself and not interacting with one or more persons. For example, if the child is trying to bounce a ball against a wall back and forth, he or she is competing with such natural forces as gravity and air pressure. Of course the child could also be interacting with natural forces when playing with others.

Over a period of many years, psychologists and others have advanced various theories of play in their study of human behavior. In general, these theories can be classified as the classical and dynamic theories. The classical theories attempt to explain why people play, while the dynamic theories are more concerned with the process of play. It is interesting to note that one of the recent dynamic theories conceives of play as being caused by the normal processes that produce learning. I subscribe wholeheartedly to this learning theory, and subsequent discussions in the book will focus upon this particular aspect of play. (The following chapter will go into detail with regard to the theory of active play.)

Ordinarily, writers on the subject of active play make more or less specific classifications of its various forms. I prefer the classifications of (1) active games, (2) rhythmic play, and (3) stunt play.

ACTIVE GAMES

For purposes of discussion here I will consider active games as active interactions of children in competitive and/or cooperative situation. As in the case of active play this description places emphasis on active games rather than passive games. I consider passive games to be card and board games where there is little physical response on the part of participants.

Games play a very important part in our society. The unique quality of games and their application to situations in everyday living have become a part of various colloquial expressions. In many instances descriptive word phrases from games have become a part of daily vocabulary and appear frequently in news articles and other written material. These words and phrases are used to describe a situation that is so familiar in a game situation that they give a clear meaning to an event from real life.

Many of us have used, at one time or another, the expression, "that's the way the ball bounces" to refer to a situation in which the outcome was not as desirable as was anticipated. Or, "that's par for the course," meaning that the difficulty was anticipated and the results were no better or no worse than expected. When we are "home free" we tend to refer to having gotten out of a tight situation, with results better than expected. The expression "the bases are loaded" describes a situation in which a critical point has been reached and there is much at stake on the next event or series of events. If you have "two strikes against you," you are operating at a grave disadvantage, and if someone "strikes out," he has failed.

It is interesting to consider how the game preferences of a particular country give insight into their culture, and this has been an important area of study and research by sociologists in recent years. The national games, the popular games, and the historical games in which the people of a nation engage provide insight into their culture. They are as much a cultural expression as their books, theater, and art.

The value of games as an important intellectual influence has been recognized for decades. For example, as far back as 1909, Bancroft[1] observed that as a child's perceptions are quickened, he sees more quickly that the ball is coming toward him, that he is in danger of being tagged, or that it is his turn; he hears footsteps behind him, or his name or number called; he feels the touch on the shoulder; or, in innumerable other ways he is aroused to quick and direct recognition of, and response to, things that go on around him.

The physiological value of games has often been ex-tolled because of the vigorous physical nature of many game activities in which children participate. And in more recent years a great deal of credence has been put in the potentialities for modifying human behavior within a social frame of reference which many games tend to provide. For example, it is possible that the game is probably the child's first social relationship with strangers and his or her first testing of self against others.

Competition and Cooperation in Games

It should be recalled that my description of active games took into account both cooperative and competitive situations. In view of the fact that there has been a considerable amount of interest in competition activities for children, it seems appropriate to discuss this, particularly as it relates to games.

It is interesting that the terms cooperation and competition are antonymous; therefore, the reconciliation of children's competitive needs and cooperative needs is not an easy matter. In a sense we are confronted with an ambivalent condition which, if not carefully handled, could place children in a state of conflict. This was recognized many decades ago when Horney[2] suggested that on the one hand everything is done to spur us toward success, which means that we must not only be assertive by aggressive, able to push others out of the way. On the other hand, we are deeply imbued with ideals, which declare that it is selfish to want anything for ourselves, that we should be humble, turn the other hand, and be yielding. Thus, modern society not only rewards one kind of behavior (cooperation) but its direct opposite (competition). Perhaps more often than not our cultural demands sanction these rewards without provision of clear-cut standards of value with regard to specific conditions under which these forms of behavior might well be practiced. Hence, the child is placed in somewhat of a quandary as to when to compete and when to cooperate.

More recently it has been found that competition does not necessarily lead to peak performance and may in fact interfere with achievement. In this connection, Kohn[3] reported on a survey on the effects of competition on sports, business, and classroom achievement and found that 65 studies showed that cooperation promoted higher achievement than competition, eight showed the reverse and 36 showed no statistically significant difference. It was concluded that the trouble with competition is that it makes one person's success depend on another's failure, and as a result when success depends on sharing resources, competition can get in the way.

In generalizing on the basis of available evidence with regard to the subject of competition, it seems justifiable to formulate the following concepts.

1. Very young children in general are not very competitive but become more so as they grow older.
2. There is a wide variety in competition among children ; that is, some are violently competitive, while others are mildly competitive, and still others are not competitive at all.
3. Boys tend to be more competitive than girls.
4. Competition should be adjusted so that there is not a preponderant number of winners over losers.
5. Competition and rivalry produce results in effort and speed of accomplishment.

In any teaching-learning situation one might be guided by the above concepts. As far as active games are concerned they are not only a good medium for the various aspects of growth and development of children but, under skillful guidance they can also provide for competitive needs of children in a pleasurable and enjoyable way.

Organization of Game Activities

The benefits that can be derived from participation in game activities are more likely to accrue when these activities are properly organized. The following discussion will focus upon general organization and signaling.

General Organization

Many games begin from certain standard formations, which include circles, lines, and rows. In a circle formation children ordinarily stand facing inward toward the center. The adult leader should be a part of the circle rather than in the center of it so as to be able to see and be seen by all children. Forming a circle of young children for the first time can be done by the leader taking the hand of another. The leader "circles around" and takes the hand of the last child to form the circle. After the children understand the concept of a circle the leader can ordinarily just tell them to arrange themselves in a circle. Circles may be made larger by each child taking a specific number of steps backward, and smaller by taking steps forward.

In some cases games played from a circle have been much maligned on the basis that there is too much inactivity of children just standing in a circle. It is doubtful if such criticism is entirely justified because the skillful leader can conduct this type of activity in such a way that there will be equal opportunity for participation. Leaders should guard against having a circle too large in those kinds of games that involve only two children as principal performers at one time. Small circles can afford many more turns.

Some feel that the circle formation has a positive psychological effect in that it tends to provide a spirit of unity among participants. That is, each player can see and become aware of the performance of other players in the group.

It is interesting to note that holding hands in a circle has important connotations for social interaction through tactile communication. Some writers have called attention to the possibilities of this by suggesting that better human relations can be obtained through intrinsic tactile communication in the utilization of activities requiring touch. In fact some studies have shown that such tactile communication provides a basis for the attraction that is necessary for black and white children to form positive relationships. More specifically, it has been demonstrated that recorded instances of tactile interaction black and white children were equivalent to those between white children and white children.

In a line formation the children stand side by side to form a line. When they have learned the idea of a line the leader can get them into this formation by merely telling them to make as many lines as needed after they have been divided into the appropriate number of groups for a given activity. The same can be said for the row formation where the children stand one behind the other.

In any kind of formation the leader should be alert to a lack of interest on the part of the participants. This is usually observed when some children are not offered the opportunity to participate because of too large a number of players. This situation can be avoided to a certain extent by such practices as having several runners and/or chasers rather than just one, and putting more than one ball into play when practical where directions for play call for only one ball.

Signaling

As in any kind of human endeavor, every game has a beginning and an ending. All games begin with some sort of signal, but there are different ways in which a game can end. A game can be played for a specific amount of time or it can continue until a particular objective has been accomplished. In some instances it may be necessary to stop a game before its completion and this requires some sort of signal.

Generally speaking, signals used in games can be broadly classified as natural signals and mechanical signals. An example of a natural starting signal would be in a game such as one called Hill Dill. The signal to start the game is "Hill Dill run over the hill." The first few words tend to get the attention of the players and the last word "hill" starts the game.

If a game does not have a particular statement or saying to get it started, the leader or a child can get it started by simply saying, "Ready!" "Go!" The word "ready" gets the attention and the word "go" starts the game.

Mechanical signals require some sort of device and can be further classified into sight and sound signals. An example of a sight signal is the use of a flag or piece of cloth. Sometimes such sight signaling devices can be of different colors and waved in different ways so as to have specific meaning for children.

The most common sounding device used for signaling is a whistle, although signaling with a horn or bell can also be used. Ordinarily, the use of mechanical signals can be kept to a minimum for starting and stopping games. If a sounding device such as a whistle is used at all, it is perhaps best to use it only for stopping activities. Children then become accustomed to associating the sound of the whistle with stopping activity. If a whistle is used both to start and stop games, confusion can sometimes result.

RHYTHMIC PLAY

The term rhythm is derived from the Greek word "rhythmos" which means "measured motion." One of the most desirable media for child expression through movement is found in rhythmic activities. One need look only to the functions of the human body to see the importance of rhythm in the life of the child. The heartbeats in rhythm, the digestive processes function in rhythm, breathing is done in rhythm; in fact, almost anything in which human beings are involved is done in a more or less rhythmic pattern.

Classification of Rhythmic Play Activities

One approach to the classification of rhythmic play activities centers around the kinds of rhythmic experiences that one might want children to have. It is recommended here that these experiences consist of (1) unstructured experiences, (2) semi-structured experiences, (3) structured experiences. It should be understood that in this particular way of grouping rhythmic experiences a certain amount of overlapping will occur as far as degree of structuring is concerned. That is, although an experience is classified as an unstructured one, there could possibly be some small degree of structuring in certain kinds of situations. With this idea in mind the following descriptions of these three types of rhythmic experiences are submitted.

Unstructured experiences include those in which there is an original or creative response and in which there has been little, if any, previous explanation or discussion in the form of specific directions. The semi-structured experiences include those in which certain movements or interpretations are suggested by the adult leader, a child, or a group of children. Structured experiences involve the more difficult rhythmic patterns associated with various types of dances. A well-balances program of rhythmic play activities should provide opportunities for these various types of rhythmic experiences.

Accompaniment for Rhythmic Play Activities

There are many different forms of accompaniment that are suitable for use with rhythmic play activities. All of these can be useful when employed under the right conditions. At the same time all of them have certain disadvantages. In the final analysis it will be up to the adult leader to select the form of accompaniment that will best meet the needs in a particular situation.

Five forms of accompaniment for rhythmic play activities are presented here along with what might be considered as advantages and disadvantages of each.

1. Clapping as a form of accompaniment can be useful in helping children gain a better understanding of tempo. There is also something to be said of the child actually becoming a part of the accompaniment on a physical basis since it gives him or her a feeling of more involvement. This is particularly important in the early stages when rhythmic activities are being introduced. Clapping can be done with the hands or by slapping various parts of the body such as the thighs or knees. A major disadvantage of clapping as a form of accompaniment is that it is virtually impossible to obtain a melody through this procedure.

2. Various kinds of percussion instruments may be used as accompaniment, the most prominent being the drum. The drum is an instrument which is easy to learn to play and the person furnishing the accompaniment can change the tempo as he or she wishes. Actually some kinds of dances, such as some of the Indian dances, require the use of the drum as accompaniment. Likewise, as in the case of clapping, the use of a drum makes it difficult to have a melody with the accompaniment.

3. Singing as a form of accompaniment is ordinarily required in movement songs and in square dances where singing calls are used. All children can become involved as in the case of clapping. One of the disadvantages of singing as a form of accompaniment is that the singing voices may become weaker as the child participates in the activity. For example, it is difficult for the child to do both tasks of singing and skipping for a very long period of time.

4. At one time the piano was a very popular form of accompaniment for rhythmic play activities. The chief disadvantage of the piano is that it is difficult instrument to learn to play and all adult leaders have not accomplished this ability. Another disadvantage is that even though one is an accomplished pianist, the player must obviously be at the

piano and thus away from the activity. The piano has an advantage in that melody can be obtained with it.

5. Perhaps the most popular form of accompaniment is recordings. Sources of this form of accompaniment are so plentiful that almost any kind of accompaniment is available. One of the distinct disadvantages of recordings concerns those that furnish instructions intended for children. Sometimes these instructions are confusing and too difficult for young children to understand. The adult leader should evaluate such instructions as determine if the above is the case. If it is found that the instructions are too difficult for a particular group of children, the adult leader can use just the musical accompaniment. The major advantage of recordings is that they are professionally prepared. However, adult leaders might well consider using a tape recorder to record their own music or singing voices of children as forms of accompaniment.

Creative Rhythms

Creative experience involves self-expression. It is concerned with the need to experiment, to express original ideas, to think, to react. Creativity and childhood enjoy a congruous relationship, in that children are naturally creative. They imagine. They pretend. They are uninhibited. They are not only original but actually ingenious in their thoughts and actions. Indeed, creativity is a characteristic inherent in the lives of practically all children. It may range from some children who create as a natural form of expression without adult stimulation to others who may need varying degrees of adult guidance and encouragement.

Such forms of creative expression as art, music, and writing are considered the traditional approaches to creative expression. However, the very essence of creative expression is movement. Movement as a form of creativity utilizes the body as the instrument of expression. For the young child the most natural form of creative expression is movement. Because of their very nature, children have an inclination for movement and they use this medium as the basic form of creative expression. Movement is the child's universal language, a most important form of communication and a most meaningful way of learning.

There are various ways to sub-classify creative rhythms. The two sub-classifications suggested here are designated as dramatization and individual interpretation. The essential difference between the two is in the degree of structuring of the activities. Dramatization centers around some sort of story, plan, or idea that can provide various kinds of clues for children, while individual interpretation has little if any structuring and involves children moving in a way the accompaniment makes them feel. That is, the ideas for movement are supposed to originate with the children.

Dramatization can involve (1) a story or idea that the children already know about or something with which they are familiar; (2) a story made up by the adult leader; or (3) a story started by the adult leader and added to by the children. An example of the first one above would be using the familiar story of "Jack and the Beanstalk," with children acting it out to drum accompaniment furnished by the adult leader.

As mentioned, in individual interpretation, ideas for movement originate with the children. Although some children might be influenced by others, the movements that each child makes to the accompaniment are likely to be unique and different from other members of the group.

Individual interpretation might be perceived in the following manner. The accompaniment is received through the auditory sense. It is "siphoned" through the human organism and nervous system and the child reacts with a movement which expresses the way the accompaniment makes him or her feel.

One of the most important aspects of individual interpretation lies in the selection of the proper kind of accompaniment. This is to say that accompaniment should be sensitive enough to depict different kinds of moods for the physical expression of one's feelings.

Movement Songs

Movement songs were traditionally referred to as singing games. This designation, however, is changing, at least in the literature where there seems to be more of a trend to refer to this form of rhythmic play as movement songs. One reason why the term singing games is losing favor in present-day terminology is that few of the songs can accurately be called games.

Movement songs are actually like dances but with relatively simple patterns that children perform to their own singing accompaniment or, as in the case of recorded accompaniment, when the singing is provided by others. The following is one way to classify these kinds of activities.

1. Those which enact simple stories or imitate the actions of everyday life.
2. Those which are based on familiar nursery rhymes or folktales.
3. Those which involve choosing partners.
4. Those in which children follow the leader in improvising rhythmic actions.

Dances

There are many ways to classify structured dances, and usually these ways are based on the philosophy of the person doing the classifying. Some people like to classify structured dances on the basis of organization; for example, circle dances, longways dances, and the like. Others might classify them according to what is done in the dance; for example, "greeting and meeting" dances. One particular thing that needs to be taken into account, regardless of the way one tends to classify structured dances, is that there will be a certain amount of overlapping in any classification.

Two broad classifications dealt with here are folk dances and square dances. Folk dances, sometimes referred to as ethnic or nationality dances, can be described as dances of a given country which have evolved nationally and spontaneously in conjunction with the everyday activities and experiences of the people who developed them. The dance patterns are performed in group formation and range from simple to rather complex forms. For the most part folk dances used in American schools have been derived from Great Britain and Europe, although some have their origin in our own country.

Square dancing appears to be uniquely American in origin. It is sometimes referred to as American country dancing or Western dancing. The square dance gets its name from the starting position of the dancers which is that of a quadrille or square.

STUNT PLAY

Stunt play is concerned predominantly with certain kinds of imitations and the performance of a variety of kinds of feat that utilize such abilities as balance, coordination, flexibility, agility, and strength. Also included are various kinds of body rolls and springs that encourage the development of these same abilities.

At the primary school level children should be given the opportunity to participate in stunt play activities commensurate with their ability. Stunts which involve imitations of animals are of great interest to boys and girls at this age level. Activities which involve some of the simple rolls are also suitable.

Stunt play at the intermediate school level should be somewhat more advanced, provided the child has had previous experience at the primary school level. Activities that involve more advance rolls and various kinds of body springs may be successfully introduced. In a like manner, more difficult kinds of balance stands may be used in the stunt play program.

Some Values of Stunt Play Activities

One of the major values ordinarily attributed to stunt play activities is their specific contributions to such elements of physical fitness as strength, agility, coordination, and flexibility. Zealous proponents of stunt play activities stoutly maintain that contributions to these various factors are more likely to accrue through these activities than may be case through games and rhythmic activities. The reason for this lies in the fact that successful performance of certain of the stunt play activities require involvement of many elements of physical fitness.

It has also been suggested that some of these kinds of activities help to build courage, confidence, and poise in children, although this is difficult to evaluate objectively.

An important value of stunt play activities, but one that is often overlooked, is the contribution that might be made to tactile perception. In this regard it has suggested that through such activities where the body touches the surface area, the child is given the opportunity to explore the environment "tactilely" with the various body segments.

NOTES

[1] Bancroft, Jessie H., *Games*, New York, The Macmillan Company, 1909.
[2] Horney, Karen, *The Neurotic Personality of Our Times*. New York, W. W. Norton & Company, Inc., 1937.
[3] Kohn A. *No Contest: The Case Against Competition*, Boson, Houghton-Mifflin Co., 1986.

Chapter 4

THE THEORY OF LEARNING
THROUGH ACTIVE PLAY

The concept of learning through active play is not new, having been around for centuries. Many philosophers of the past who advocated this approach to learning did not have the benefit of scientific experimentation. In modern times, however, some individuals, including the present author, have attempted to build an objective base under this long-held theoretical postulation by means of experimental research.

It has been reported that the idea may go back more than 5,000 years. For instance one source[1] indicates that Plato in his writing praised the ancient Egyptian method of teaching arithmetic by means of play. In fact, Plato himself in The Republic in 370 B. C. indicated that "Learning takes place best through play and play situations." He also suggested that, "Lessons have been invented for the merest infants to learn, by way of play and fun." And, almost three centuries ago Francois Fenelon, the famous French educator and ecclesiastic, is reputed to have suggested that he had seen certain children who had learned to read while playing.

No question about it, throughout the ages the concept of learning through active play has been held in high esteem by many outstanding philosophers and educators. Such pronouncements extend over several centuries from Plato's assertations to a modern 20th century statement by L. P. Jacks that "the discovery of the educational possibilities of the play side of life may be counted one of the greatest discoveries of the present day."

One of the main reasons for going into a rather detailed discussion of the theory of child learning through active play is based on the idea that some people tend to be skeptical about this approach to learning. Possibly the reason for this is that so many individuals tend to associate learning only with work. They seem to feel that children can learn only when "bent over a book." Perhaps the following discussions might help to dispel this notion.

Active play learning is based on the theory that children, being predominantly movement oriented, will learn better when what might arbitrarily be called academic learning takes place through pleasurable physical activity. That is, when the motor component (active play) operates at a maximal level in skill development in the 3Rs that has essentially be oriented to verbal learning. This is not to say that active play learning and verbal learning are two mutually exclusive kinds of learning. It is recognized that in verbal learning, which involves almost complete abstract symbolic manipulations, there may be, among others, such motor components as tension, sub-vocal speech, and physiological changes in metabolism, which operate at a minimal level. It is also recognized that in active play where the learning is predominantly motor in nature, verbal learning is evident, although perhaps at a minimal level. For example, when a child learns through the active play medium there is a certain amount of verbalization (talking) in developing a "muscle sense" concept of the particular active play experience that is to be used.

This procedure of learning through active play involves the selection of an activity such as an active game, rhythm, or stunt which is taught to the child and used as a learning activity for the development of an academic skill. An attempt is made to arrange an active play learning situation so that a fundamental intellectual skill is practiced or rehearsed in the course of participating in the active play experience.

Although a large number of examples are presented in subsequent chapters, it seems appropriate to give an example of such an experience at this point. The example that will be used for this purpose is a stunt play activity called Move like Animals. The adult leader can begin by reading the following to the child.

We try to move like animal. We move like a bear. We move like an elephant. We move like a frog. We will try to move like these animals. We will take five steps like a bear. We will take four steps like an elephant. We will take two jumps like a frog. Now we will do it the other way. Two jumps like a frog. Four steps like an elephant. Five steps like a bear.

The child proceeds by creating the various animal walks under the guidance of the adult leader. The following mathematics skills and concepts are built-in ingredients of this activity.

1. Rational counting. This means calling numbers in sequence 1, 2, 3, etc.
2. Cardinal number ideas. Cardinal numbers are used in simple counting, and they indicate how many elements there are in a given assemblage –1, 5, 15, etc. (Ordinal numbers are used to show order or succession – 1st, 2nd, 3rd, etc.)
3. Addition.
4. Commutative law. This means that the same total is arrived at regardless of the order in which the numbers are arranged: 2 plus 4 equals 6, and 4 plus 2 equals 6.

Following are some suggestions that an adult leader might consider in using the preceding active play experience. The adult should be sure to take into account the ability level of the child.

1. The child can count the animal movements as he or she makes them. Also the child can add with the help of the adult to find how many movements there were altogether.
2. To use the cardinal number idea, after the child has taken five steps like a bear, the adult can ask, "How many steps did you take?"
3. To reinforce the understanding of the commutative law the adult can put 5 + 4 + 2 and 2 + 4 + 5 on cards for the child to see before and/or after the activity.

The above suggestions do not include all of the possibilities that can be used with this sample activity, and the creative adult will obviously think of numerous others.

FACTORS THAT MAKE LEARNING
EASIER THROUGH ACTIVE PLAY

During the early school year and at ages six to eight particularly, it is likely that learning is frequently limited by a relatively short attention span rather than only by intellectual capabilities. Moreover, some children who do not appear to learn well in abstract terms can more readily grasp concepts when given an opportunity to use them in an applied manner. Since the child is a creature of movement, and also likely to deal better in concrete rather than abstract terms, it would seem to follow naturally that the active play learning medium is well suited for him or her.

As mentioned previously, the preceding statement should not be interpreted to mean that I am suggesting that learning through active play experiences (motor learning) and passive learning experiences (verbal learning) are two different kinds of learning. The position is taken here that learning is learning, even though in the active play approach the motor component may be operating at a higher level than in most of the traditional types of learning activities.

The theory of learning accepted here is that learning takes place in terms of reorganization of the systems of perception (such as seeing and hearing) into a functional and integrated whole because of the result of certain stimuli. This implies, as mentioned in Chapter 1 that problem solving is a very desirable and worthwhile way of human learning. In an active play situation that is well planned by the adult leader a great deal of consideration should be given to the built-in possibilities for learning in terms of problem solving.

Another very important factor to consider with respect to the active play learning medium is that a considerable part of the learning of young children is motor in character, with the child devoting a good proportion of attention to skills of a movement nature. Furthermore, learning of a movement nature tend to use up a large amount of the young child's time and energy and are often associated with other learning. In addition it is well known by experienced classroom teachers at the primary level that the child's motor mechanism is active to the extent that it is almost an impossibility to remain for very long periods in a quiet state.

The comments made thus far have been concerned with some of the general aspects of the value of the active play learning medium. The following discussions will focus more specifically on certain factors in the active play learning medium that is very much in line with child learning. These factors are motivation, muscle sense, and reinforcement, all of which are somewhat interdependent and interrelated.

The Motivational Factor

Motivation can be thought of as something that causes a person to act. It is concerned with why people do certain things. What, how, when, and where a person does something is easy to determine. On the other hand, why one acts in a certain way is not so easy to observe. Thought of in these terms, motivation could be considered as something that gives direction to one's behavior.

For the purpose of this discussion we should take into account what I will arbitrarily call outside and inside motivation. Outside motivation can be described as applying incentives that are external to a given activity so that performance may be improved. Inside motivation means that a given activity is exciting enough for a person to engage in it for the purpose of enjoyment derived from the activity itself.

Outside motivation has been and continues to be used as a means of spurring individuals to achievement. This most often takes the form of various kinds of reward incentives. The main objection to this type of motivation is that it may tend to focus the learner's attention upon the reward rather than the learning task and the total learning situation.

People are motivated for different reasons. In general, the child is motivated when he or she discovers what seems to be a suitable reason for engaging in a certain activity. The most valid reason, of course, is that the child sees a purpose for the activity and derives enjoyment from it. The child must feel that what is being done is important and purposeful. When this occurs and the child gets the impression of success in a given situation, the motivation is within the activity (inside motivation). It comes about naturally as a result of the child's interest in the activity. It is the premise here that active play learning contains this built-in ingredient so necessary to desirable and worthwhile learning.

The following discussions of this section of the chapter will be concerned with two aspects of motivation that are considered to be an important part of the active play learning medium. These are motivation in relation to interest and motivation in relation to knowledge of results.

Motivation in Relation to Interest

It is important to have an understanding of the meaning of interest as well as an appreciation of how interests function as an aid to learning. Described simply, interest is a state of being, a way of reacting to a certain situation. Interests are those areas to which a child reacts with interest over an extended period of time.

It was stated in Chapter 1 (as a principle of learning) that a good condition for learning is a situation in which a child agrees with and acts upon the learning that he or she considers of most value. This means that the child accepts as most valuable those things, which are of greatest interest. To the very large majority of children, active play experiences are likely to be of the greatest personal value.

Under most circumstances a very high interest level is maintained in active play experiences simply because of the expectation of pleasure that children tend to associate with such activities. The structure of a learning activity is directly related to the length of time the learning act can be tolerated by the learner without loss of interest. Active play experiences by their very nature are more likely to be so structured than are many of the traditional learning activities.

Motivation in Relation to Knowledge of Results

Knowledge of results is commonly referred to as feedback. It has been recognized for years that feedback is the process of providing the learner with information as to how accurate his or her reactions were. Psychologists usually refer to feedback as knowledge of various kinds that the performer received about his or her performance.

Many learning theorists agree that knowledge of results is the strongest, most important aspect controlling performance and learning and, further, those studies have repeatedly shown that there is no improvement without it, progressive improvement with it and deterioration after its withdrawal. In fact, there appears to be a sufficient abundance of objective evidence that indicates that learning is usually more effective when one receives some immediate information on how he or she is progressing. It would appear rather obvious that such knowledge of results is an important aid to learning because one would have little idea of which of his or her responses were correct. Some psychologists compare it to trying to learn a task while blindfolded.

The active play learning medium provides almost instant knowledge of results because the child can actually see and feel involvement in the activity. He or she does not become the victim of a poorly constructed paper-and-pencil test, the results of which may have little or no meaning for the child.

The Muscle Sense Factor

Earlier in this chapter it was stated that the theory of learning accepted here is that learning takes place in terms of reorganization of the systems of perception into a functional and integrated whole as a result of certain stimuli. These systems of perception, or sensory processes as they are sometimes referred to, are ordinarily considered to consist of the senses of sight, hearing, touch, smell, and taste. Even though this point of view is convenient for most purposes, it no doubt greatly simplifies the ways by which information can be fed into the human organism. A number of sources of sensory input are overlooked particularly the senses that enable the body to maintain its correct posture. In fact the 60 to 70 pounds of muscle, which includes more than 600 in number, that are attached to the skeleton of the average-sized man could well be his most important sense organ.

Various estimates indicate that the visual sense brings us more than three-fourths of our knowledge. Therefore, it could be said with little reservation that man is eye-minded. However, it could be that a larger portion of the nervous system is devoted to receiving and integrating sensory input originating in the muscles and joint structures than is devoted to the eye and ear combined. In view of this it could also be contended that man is muscle sense minded.

The scientific term for muscle sense is proprioception. At the risk of becoming too technical, I nevertheless should mention that the proprioceptors are sensory nerve terminals that give information concerning movements and position of the body. A proprioceptive feedback mechanism is involved, which in a sense regulates movement. Since children are so movement oriented, it appears a reasonable speculation that proprioceptive feedback from the receptors of muscles, skin, and joints may contribute to learning when active play is used to develop skills in reading, mathematics, and writing.

The Reinforcement Factor

In considering the relationship of active play learning to reinforcement theory, the meaning of reinforcement needs to be taken into account. An acceptable general description of reinforcement is that there is increase in the efficiency of a response to a stimulus brought about by the concurrent action of another stimulus. A simple example of this would be when the adult leader gives praise and encouragement when the child is engaged in a task. Generally, the same principle applies when athletes refer to the "home court advantage," that is; the home fans are present to spur them on. The basis for contending that active play learning is consistent with general reinforcement theory is that it reinforces attention to the learning task and learning behavior. It keeps the child involved in the learning activity, which is the major application for reinforcement procedures. Moreover, there is perhaps little in the way of human behavior that is not reinforced, or at least reinforcible, by the feedback of some sort. The importance of muscle sense (proprioceptive) feedback has already been discussed in this particular regard.

In summarizing this discussion it would appear that active play learning generally establishes a more effective situation for learning for the following reasons:

1. The greater motivation of the child in the active play learning situation involves emphasis on those behaviors directly concerned with the learning activities.
2. The muscle sense emphasis in active play learning involves a greater number of responses associated with and conditioned to learning stimuli.
3. The gratifying aspects of active play learning provide a generalized situation of reinforcers for learning.

EVIDENCE TO SUPPORT THE THEORY

Any approach to learning should be based at least to some degree upon objective evidence produced by experimental research, and this is the subject of the following discussion.

There are a number of acceptable ways of studying how behavioral changes take place in children. In this regard, over a period of several years I have conducted numerous controlled studies concerned with the active play approach to learning. My findings are suggestive enough to give rise to some interesting conclusions, which may be briefly summarized as follows:

1. In general, children tend to learn certain 3Rs skills better through the active play learning medium than many of the traditional approaches.
2. The active play approach, while favorable to both boys and girls, appears to be more favorable for boys.
3. When active play learning experiences are compared to passive play learning experiences (such as card games and board games), the active play approach is shown to be more favorable for both boys and girls.
4. The active play approach appears to be more favorable for children with average and below average intelligence.
5. For children with higher levels of intelligence, it may be possible to introduce more advanced concepts at an earlier age through the active play learning medium.

In addition to the above scientific findings, the many successful experiences with the field tested active play learning experiences recommended in this book should encourage parents, teachers, and other adults to use the approach in an effort to help children learn about the 3Rs through pleasurable and enjoyable experiences.

NOTE

[1] Painter, F. V. N., *A History of Education*, New York, D. Appleton and Co., 1896, p. 34.

Chapter 5

CONDUCTING THE ACTIVE
PLAY LEARNING EXPERIENCE

It should be obvious that the success of active play learning will depend in a large degree upon how well the experiences are presented. This is the reason for providing a detailed account of the procedure in this chapter.

The term teacher in the present discussion refers to any adult who will assume the responsibility for conducting active play learning experiences.

The teacher should be aware that every child is almost incredibly unique and that he or she approaches all learning tasks with his or her own level of motivation, capacity, experience, and vitality. Moreover, the teacher must by a combination of emotional and logical appeal, help each individual find his or her own way through the experience and at his or her own rate. The teacher must also help the individual "nail down" the meaning of the experience and help to incorporate it and its use into the child's own life.

The teacher's role should be that of a guide who supervises and directs desirable active play learning experiences. In providing such experiences, the teacher should constantly keep in mind how an activity can contribute to the physical, social, emotional, and intellectual development of the child. This implies that the teacher should develop an understanding of the principles of learning presented in Chapter 1, and to apply these principles properly in presenting active play learning experiences.

It is important that the teacher recognize that individual differences exist among teachers as well as children and that some of these differences will influence their teaching methods. Sometimes one teacher may have greater success than another with a method. This implies that there should be no specified resolute method of teaching for all teachers. On the other hand, teachers should allow themselves to deviate from recommended conformity if they are able to provide desirable learning experiences through a method peculiar to their own abilities. This, of course, means that the procedures used should be compatible with conditions under which learning takes place best.

CHARACTERISTICS OF GOOD TEACHERS

Over the years there have been numerous attempts to identify objectively those characteristics of good teachers that set them apart from average or poor teachers. Obviously, this is a difficult matter because of the countless variables involved.

It is entirely possible for two teachers to have the same degree of intelligence and understanding of what they are teaching. Yet, it is also possible that one of these teachers will consistently achieve good results with children, while the other will not have much success. Perhaps a good part of the reason for this difference in success lies in those individual differences of teachers that relate to certain personality factors and how they deal and interact with children. Based upon the available research and numerous interviews with both teachers and children, I have found the following characteristics tend to emerge most often among good teachers.

1. Good teachers possess those characteristics that in one way or another have a humanizing effect on children. An important factor of good teachers that appeals to most children is a sense of humor.
2. In all cases, good teachers are fair and democratic in their dealings with children and tend to maintain the same positive feelings toward the so-called "problem" child as they do with other children.
3. Another very important characteristic is that good teachers are able to relate easily to children. They have the ability and sensitivity to "listen through children's ears and see through children's eyes."
4. Good teachers are flexible. They know that different approaches need to be used with different groups of children as well as individual children. In addition, good teacher can adjust easily to changing situations.

5. Good teachers have control. Different teachers exercise control in different ways, but good teachers tend to have a minimum of control problems because they provide a learning environment where control becomes a minimum problem.

TEACHING AND LEARNING IN ACTIVE PLAY

The teaching-learning process is complicated and complex. For this reason it is important that teachers have as full an understanding as possible of the role of teaching and learning in active play.

Basic Considerations

The concepts of learning that a teacher subscribes to are directly related to the kind and variety of active play learning experiences and activities that will be provided for children. Thus, it is important for teachers to explore some of the factors that make for the most desirable and worthwhile learning. Among the factors that should help to orient the reader with regard to some basic understandings in the teaching of active play activities are: (1) an understanding of the meaning of certain terms, (2) an understanding of the derivation of teaching methods, and (3) an understanding of the various learning products in active play.

Meaning of Terms

Due to the fact that certain terms, because of their multiple use, do not actually have a universal definition, no attempt will be made here to define terms. On the other hand, it will be the purpose to describe certain terms rather than attempt to define them. The reader should view descriptions of terms that follow with this general idea in mind.

Learning. Although this term was described in Chapter 1, it appears appropriate to do so again here for purposes of continuity. Most descriptions of learning are characterized by the idea that learning involves some sort of change in the individual. This means that when an individual has learned, behavior is modified in one or more ways. Thus, a valid criterion for learning would be that after having an experience, a person could behave in a way in which he or she could not have behaved before having the experience.

Teaching. Several years ago I was addressing a group of teachers on the subject of teaching and learning. Introducing the discussion in somewhat abstract terms, I asked, "What is teaching?" After a short period of embarrassing deliberation, one member of the group interrogated the following answer with some degree of uncertainty: "Is it imparting information?" This kind of thinking is characteristic of the traditional meaning of the term teaching. A more acceptable description would be to think of it in terms of guidance, direction, and supervision of behavior that results in desirable and worthwhile learning. This is to say that it is the job of the teacher to guide the child's learning rather than to impart to him or her a series of unrelated and sometimes meaningless facts.

Method. The term method might be considered as an orderly and systematic means of achieving an objective. In other words, method is concerned with "how to do" something in order to achieve desired results. If best results are to be obtained for children in their active play experiences, it becomes necessary that the most desirable active play learning experiences be provided. Consequently, it becomes essential that teachers use all of the ingenuity and resourcefulness at their command in the proper direction and guidance of these learning experiences. The procedures that teachers use are known as teaching methods.

Derivation of Teaching Methods

Beginning teachers often ask, "Where do we get our ideas for teaching methods?" For the most part this question should be considered in general terms. Although there are a variety of acceptable teaching procedures, all of these are likely to be derived from two somewhat broad sources.

The first of these involves an accumulation of knowledge of educational psychology and what is known about the learning process in providing for active play learning experiences. The other is the practices of successful teachers.

In most instances, preparation of prospective teachers includes at least some study of educational psychology as it applies to the learning process and certain accepted principles of learning. With this basic information it is expected that beginning teachers have sufficient knowledge to make application of it in the practical situation.

It has been my observation over a period of years that many beginning teachers tend to rely too much upon the practices of successful teachers as a source of teaching methods. The validity of this procedure is based on the assumption that such successful practices are likely to have as their bases the application of fundamental psychological principles of learning. Nevertheless, it should be the responsibility of every teacher to become familiar with the basic psychological principles of learning and to attempt to apply these in the best possible way when providing the most desirable and worthwhile active play learning experiences for children.

PHASES OF THE TEACHING-LEARNING SITUATION

There are certain fundamental phases involved in almost every active play teaching-learning situation. These are (1) auditory input, (2) visual input, (3) participation, and (4) evaluation. Although these four phases are likely to be weighted in various degrees, they will occur in the teaching of practically every active play situation regardless of the type of activity that is being taught. While the application of the various phases may be of a general nature, they nevertheless should be utilized in such as way that they become specific in a particular situation. Depending upon the type of activity, the use and application of the various phases should be characterized by flexibility and awareness of the objectives of the situation.

Auditory-Input Phase

The term auditory may be described as stimulation occurring through the organs of hearing. The term input is concerned with the use of as many media as are deemed necessary for a particular teaching-learning situation. The term output is concerned with behaviors or reactions of the learner resulting from the various forms of input. Auditory input involves the various learning media that are directed to the auditory sense. This should not be interpreted to mean that the auditory-input phase is a one-way process. While much of such input may originate with the teacher, consideration should also be given to the verbal interaction among children and between children and the teacher.

Active play provides a most desirable opportunity for learning through direct, purposeful experience. In other words, the active play learning situation is "learning by doing," or learning through pleasurable physical activity. Although verbalization might well be kept to a minimum, a certain amount of auditory input, which provides for auditory association, appears to be essential for a satisfactory teaching-learning situation. The quality of "kinesthetic feel" may be described as the process of changing ideas into muscular action and is of primary importance in the proper acquisition of active play skills. It might be said that the auditory-input phase helps to set the stage for a kinesthetic concept of the particular activity being taught.

Great care should be taken with the auditory-input phase in active play teaching-learning situations. The ensuing discussions are intended to suggest to the reader ways in which the greatest benefits can accrue when using this particular learning medium.

Preparing Children for Listening

Since it is likely that the initial part of the auditory-input phase will originate with the teacher, care should be taken to prepare children for listening. The teacher may set the scene for listening by relating the activity to the interests of children. In addition, the teacher should be on the alert to help children develop their own purposes for listening.

In preparing children to listen, the teacher should be aware that it is of importance that the comfort of children be taken into consideration and that attempts should be made for removing any possible attention-distracting factors. Although evidence concerning the effect of environmental distractions on listening effectiveness is not in great abundance, there is reason to believe that distraction does interfere with listening comprehension. Moreover, it is well known that being able to see as well as hear the speaker is an important factor in listening distraction.

These factors have a variety of implications for the auditory-input phase. For example, consideration would be given to the placement of children when an active play activity requires auditory input by the teacher. This means, for instance, as mentioned previously, that if the teacher is providing auditory input from a circle formation, the teacher should take a position a part of the circle instead from speaking from the center of the circle. Also, it might be well for teachers to consider that an object, such as a ball, can become an attention-distracting factor when an activity is being discussed. The attention of the children is sometimes focused on the ball, and they may not listen to what is being said. The teacher might wish to conceal such an object until time for its use is most appropriate.

Teacher-Child and Child-Child Interaction

It was mentioned previously that the auditory-input phase is a two-way process. As such, it is important to take into account certain factor involving verbal interaction of children with children, and teacher with child.

By "democracy" some people seem to mean everyone doing or saying whatever happens to cross his or her mind at the moment. This raises the question of control, and it should be emphasized that group discussions, if they are to be democratic, must be in control. This is to say that if a group discussion is to succeed it must be under control, and let me stress that democracy implies discipline and control.

Group discussion is a kind of socio-intellectual exercise (involving numerous bodily movements, of course) just as an active game is a kind of socio-intellectual exercise (involving, too, higher mental functioning). Both imply individual discipline to keep play moving within bounds, and both require moderators (officials) overseeing, though not participating in, the play in the manner that is objective and aloof from the heat of competition. In brief, disciplined, controlled group discussion can be a training ground for living in a society in which both individual and group interests are profoundly respected – just as games can serve a comparable function.

Another important function in teacher-child interaction is with the time given to questions after the teacher has provided auditory input. The teacher should give time for questions but should be very skillful in the use of questions. It must be determined immediately whether or not a question is a legitimate one. This implies that the type of questions asked can help serve as criteria for the teacher to evaluate the auditory-input phase. For example, if numerous questions are asked, it is apparent that either the auditory input from the teachers was unsatisfactory, or the children were not paying attention.

Directionality of Sound

In summarizing recent findings concerned with the directionality of sound, a number of interesting factors important to the auditory-input phases have emerged. For example, individuals tend to initiate movements toward the direction from which the sound cue emanates. That is, if a verbal cue is given that instructs the individual to move a body segment or segments to the left, but the verbal cue emanates from the right side of the individual, the initial motor response is to the right, followed by a reverse response to the left. It is recommended that when working on direction of motor responses with children, one should make certain that sound cues come from the direction in which the motor response is made. The point is that children have enough difficulty in discriminating left from right without confusing them further.

Visual-Input Phase

Various estimates indicate that the visual sense brings us upwards of three-fourths of our knowledge. If this postulation can be used as a valid criterion, the merits of the visual-input phase in teaching about active play are readily discernible. In many cases, visual input, which should provide for visual-motor association, serves as a happy medium between verbal symbols and direct participation in helping teachers further prepare children for the kinesthetic feel mentioned previously.

In general, there are two types of visual input, which can be used satisfactorily in teaching about active play. These are visual symbols and human demonstration (live performance).

Visual Symbols

Included among the visual symbols used in active play are motion pictures and various kinds of flat or still pictures. One of the disadvantages of the latter centers around the difficulty in portraying movement with a still figure. Although movement is obtained with a motion picture, it is not depicted in third dimension, which causes some degree of ineffectiveness when this medium is used. One valuable use of visual symbols is that of employing diagrams to show the dimensions of activity areas.

Human Demonstration

Some of the guides to action in the use of demonstration follow:

1. If the teacher plans to demonstrate, this should be included in the preparation by practicing and rehearsing the demonstration.
2. The teacher does not need to do all of the demonstrating; in fact, in some cases it may be much more effective to have one or more

children demonstrate. Since the teacher might be expected to be a skilled performer, a demonstration by a child will oftentimes serve to show other children that one of their peers can perform the activity and that they should be able to do it also.

3.   A demonstration should be based on the skill and ability of a given group of children. If it appears to be too difficult for them , they might not want to attempt the activity.

4.   When at all possible, a demonstration should parallel the timing and the conditions under which it will be put to practical application. However, if the situation is one in which the movements are complex or done with great speed, it might be well to have the demonstration conducted on a slower basis than that involved in the actual performance situation.

5.   If there is a group the children should be arranged so that everyone is in a favorable position to see the demonstration. Moreover, the children should be able to view the demonstration from a position where it takes place. For example, if the activity is to be performed in a lateral plane, children should be placed so that they can see it from this position.

6.   Although auditory input and human demonstration can be satisfactorily combined in many situations, care should be taken that auditory input is not lost, because the visual sense offsets the auditory sense. That is, one should not become an attention-distracting factor for the other. It will be up to the teacher to determine the amount of verbalization that should accompany the demonstration.

7.   After the demonstration has been presented it might be a good practice to demonstrate again and have the children go trough the movements with the demonstrator. This provides for the use of the kinesthetic sense together with the visual sense that makes for close integration of the two sensory stimuli.

Participation Phase

The following considerations should be kept in mind in connection with the participation phase of teaching.

1. The practice session should be planned so that the greatest possible amount of time is given to participation.
2. If the activity does not progress as expected in the participation phase, perhaps the fault may lie in the procedures used in the auditory-input and visual-input phases. Participation then becomes a criterion for the evaluation of former phases.
3. The teacher should take into account the fact that the original attempts in learning an activity should meet with a reasonable degree of success.
4. The teacher should constantly be aware of the possibility of fatigue of children during participation and should understand that individual differences of children create a variation with regard to how rapidly fatigue takes place.
5. Participation should be worthwhile for every child.
6. During the participation phase, the teacher should constantly analyze the performance of children in order to determine those who need improvement in skills. Behaviorisms of children should be observed while they are engaging in the active play activity. For example, various types of emotional behavior might be noted in active play situations that might not be indicated in any other experience.
7. Problems involved during participation should be kept in mind for subsequent evaluation with the children.

Evaluation Phase

Evaluation is a very important phase of the active play teaching-learning situation, and yet, perhaps one of the most neglected aspects of it. For instance, it is not an uncommon procedure to have a practice session end without an evaluation of the results of the session.

Children should be given an opportunity to discuss the session and to suggest ways in which improvement might be effected. When this procedure is followed, children are placed in a problem-solving situation and desirable learning is more likely, with the teacher guiding learning rather than dominating the situation in a direction-giving type of procedure. Also more and better continuity is likely to be provided from one session to another when time is taken for evaluation. In addition, children are much more likely to develop a clearer understanding of the purposes of active play if they are given an opportunity to discuss the procedures involved.

Ordinarily, the evaluation phase should take place at the end of the session. Experience has shown that a satisfactory evaluation procedure can be effected in five to six minutes, depending upon the nature of the activity and upon what actually occurred during the session. Under certain circumstances, if an activity is not proceeding well in the participation phase, it may be desirable to stop and carry out what is known as a "spot" evaluation. This does not mean that the teacher should stop an activity every time the situations is not developing according to plan. A suggestion or hint to children who are having difficulty with performance can perhaps preclude the need for having all of the children cease participation. On the other hand, if the situation is such that the needs of the group will best be met by a discussion concerning the solution of a problem, the teacher is indeed justified in stopping the activity and conducting an evaluation "on the spot."

In concluding this chapter, let me say that if the teacher is to provide active play learning experiences that contribute to total development of children, there must be a clear perspective to the total learning that is expected from the area of active play. This implies that in order to provide for progression in active play learning there must be some means of preserving continuity from one session to another. Consequently, each individual session becomes a link in the chain of active play learning that contribute to the total development of the child. Experience has shown that the implementation of this theory into reality can be most successfully accomplished by wise and careful planning of every session.

Chapter 6

IMPROVING ABILITY TO LEARN
THROUGH ACTIVE PLAY

How does an adult go about improving a child's ability to learn? In the first place, something needs to be known about those abilities that need to be improved for desirable and worthwhile learning to take place. Generally speaking, these abilities can be classified under the broad area of perceptual-motor abilities. To understand the meaning of perceptual-motor we first need to define the term's perception and motor separately, and then derive a meaning when these two terms are combined.

Perception is concerned with how we obtain information through the senses and what we make of it. For purposes here, the term motor is concerned with the impulse of motion, resulting in a change of position through the various forms of body movement. When the two items are put together (perceptual-motor), the implication is an organization of the information received through one or more of the senses, with related voluntary motor responses.

The development of perceptual-motor abilities in children is referred to by some child development specialists as the process of providing "learning-to-learn" activities. This means improvement upon such perceptual-motor qualities as body awareness, laterality and sense of direction, auditory and visual perception skills, and kinesthetic and tactile perception skills. A deficiency in one or more of these can detract from a child's ability to learn.

It is the function of this chapter to help adults determine if such deficiencies exist, along with recommended active play experiences to help improve upon them. Even though a deficiency does not exist in any of these factors, the active play experiences suggested can still be used to sharpen and improve upon these skills, which is so important to learning.

IMPROVING BODY AWARENESS THROUGH ACTIVE PLAY

As far as this subject is concerned, there are a number of terms that have been used by different writers to convey essentially the same meaning. Among others, these include body awareness, body schema, body image, body concept, body sense, and body experience. Regardless of which term is used, they all are likely to be concerned with the ability of the child to distinguish the particular features of the body parts. I prefer to use the term body awareness for this purpose.

Most child development specialists tend to agree that a child's knowledge of the names and function of the various body parts is a very important factor in the improvement of learning ability. For example, body awareness gives a child a better understanding of the space his or her body takes and the relationships of its parts. Incidentally, these are critical factors in building foundations of mathematics competency.

It is doubtful that there are any foolproof methods of detecting problems of body awareness in children. The reason for this is that many things that are said to indicate body awareness problems can also be symptoms of other deficiencies. Nevertheless, adults should be alert to detect certain possible deficiencies.

Generally speaking, there are two ways in which deficiencies concerned with body awareness might be detected. First, some deficiencies can be noticed, at least in part, by observing certain behaviors. The following generalized list contains examples of both of these possibilities and is presented to assist the adult in this particular regard.

1. One technique often used to diagnose possible problems of body awareness is to have children make a drawing of themselves. The main reason for this is to see if certain parts of the body are not included in the drawing. Since the child's interest in drawing a man dates from earliest attempts to represent things symbolically, it is possible, through typical drawings of young children, to trace certain

characteristic stages of perceptual development. It has also been found that the procedure of drawing a picture of himself or herself assists in helping to detect if there is a lack of body awareness.

2. Sometimes the child with a lack of body awareness may show tenseness in movements. At the same time he or she may be unsure of movements in attempts to move the body segments (arm or leg).

3. If the child is instructed to move a body part such as placing one foot forward, he or she may direct attention to the body part before making the movement; or the child may look at another child to observe the movement before attempting to make the movement. (This could also be because of not understanding the instructions for the movement.)

4. When instructed to use one body part (arm) the child may move the corresponding part (other arm) when it is not necessary. For example, he or she may be asked to swing the right arm and may also start to swing the left arm at the same time.

5. In such activities as catching an object, the child may turn toward the object when it is not necessary. For example, when a thrown beanbag approaches close to the child, he or she may move forward with either side of the body rather than trying to catch the beanbag with the hands while both feet remain stationary.

ACTIVE PLAY EXPERIENCES INVOLVING BODY AWARENESS

In general, it might be said that when a child is given the opportunity to use the body freely in active play experiences, an increase in body awareness occurs. More specifically, there are certain activities that can be useful in helping children identify and understand the use of various body parts as well as the relationship of these parts. Over a period of time I have conducted a number of experiments to determine the effect of participating in certain active play experiences on body awareness. The following activities have proved to be very useful for this purpose.

Busy Bee

The adult and child stand facing each other. To begin with, the adult can be the caller. The adult makes calls such as "shoulder-to-shoulder," "toe-to-

toe," or "hand-to-hand." As the calls are made, the adult and child go through the motions with each other. After a few calls, the adult calls out "Busy Bee!" and the two of them run to a point that was previously decided on. The idea is to see who can reach the point first. This activity continues with the child being the caller. When this activity is used with a group of players, the caller stands in the middle of the activity area and makes the calls. At the signal of "Busy Bee" all player try to find a new partner, and the caller also tries to find a partner. A new caller is selected when the activity is played again.

To give the reader an idea of how such a play activity can improve upon body awareness, I report here on an experiment using this particular activity with a group of several kindergarten children. Before the activity, the children were asked to draw a picture of themselves. Many did not know how to begin, and others omitted some of the major limbs in their drawings. After playing Busy Bee, the children were asked again to draw a picture of themselves. This time they were more successful. All of the drawings had bodies, heads, arms, and legs. Some of them had hands, feet, eyes, and ears. A few even had teeth and hair.

Mirrors

To start this activity, the adult can be the leader and stands facing the child a short distance away. The adult goes through a variety of movements and the child tries to do exactly the same thing; that is, he or she acts as a mirror. The child and adult take turns being the leader. This can be done with several players by having them stand in line with the leader in front of them and going through the different movements.

In this activity the child becomes aware of different body parts and movements as the leader makes various movements. The adult should be alert to see how quickly the child is able to do the movements that are made.

Move Along

The child lies on his or her back on the floor. The adult gives a signal such as a clap of the hands, and the child moves the arms and legs in a way that he or she chooses. The adult than gives the name of a movement such as "Move your legs like a bicycle," and then gives the signal to begin the movement. This same activity can be used with several players.

The adult should observe closely to see how rapidly the child responds to the movements called. Also, if the activity is used with several players, the adult should observe to see if the child or other children are waiting to see what others are going to do before making the correct movement.

Body Tag

To start this game the child is It. He or she chases and tries to tag the adult. If the child is successful the adult becomes It. To be officially tagged, a specific part of the body must be tagged by It. Thus, the activity could be shoulder tag, arm tag, or leg tag as desired. This activity can be played with several players and is actually much more fun when there are more than two players.

The adult observes the child to see whether or not he or she tags the correct body part. To add more interest to the activity, the one who is It can call out the body part to be tagged during each session of the activity.

Squat Through

From a standing position the child assumes a squatting stance, placing the hands on the surface area to the outside of the legs with the palms flat and the fingers forward. This is count number 1. Switching the weight to the hands and arms, the child extends the legs sharply to the rear until the body is straight. The weight of the body is now on the hands and balls of the feet. This is count number 2. On count number 3 the child returns to the squatting position, and on count number 4 the child returns to the erect standing position.

The child is able to see the function of certain body parts as the weight is shifted. After directions are given for the performance of the activity, the adult can notice how well they are followed with reference to the correct position of the body parts concerned.

Snowflakes

Creative activities are highly recommended on the basis that when a child is able to use the body freely, there is a strong likelihood that there will be increased body awareness. This creative activity and those that follow are intended for this purpose. The adult reads to the child, and then with various degrees of guidance the child tries to depict the activity in the reading selection by creating his or her own responses.

Snow!
Snowflakes fall.
They fall down.
Down, down, down.
Around and around.
They fall to the ground.
Could you move like snowflakes?

Mr. Snowman and Mr. Sun

See Mr. Snowman.
See Mr. Sun.
Mr. Snowman see Mr. Sun.
Mr. Snowman is going.
Going, going, going.
Mr. Snowman is gone.
Could you do like Mr. Snowman?

Tick, Tock

Listen to the clock.
It says, "Tick, Tock" as it keeps the time.
Would you like to play you are a clock?
This is the way.
Stand up.
Hold your hands.
Keep your arms straight.

Now keep time with the clock by swinging your arms.
Ready.
Swing your arms from side to side.
Swing them to the tick tock of the clock.
Can you keep time as you move from side to side?

Automobile

Pretend you are an automobile.
Hum like the engine.
Hmm! Hmm! HMM!
Your feet are the wheels.
Hum as you go.
Can you hum while you go like an automobile?

In these activities the adult can carefully observe the movements of the child with reference to the body parts used in the creative activities. "Did you use your arms? Your legs?" and so on. If the adult desires, a drum or suitable recording can be used as accompaniment.

IMPROVING LATERALITY AND DIRECTIONALITY
THROUGH ACTIVE PLAY

The terms laterality and directionality are probably new to some readers. These qualities are concerned with distinction of the body sides and sense of direction. More specifically, laterality is an internal awareness of the left and right sides of the body in relation to the child. It is concerned with the child's knowledge of how each side of the body is used separately or together. Directionality is the projection into space of laterality. That is, the awareness of left and right, up and down, over and under, etc., in the world around the child. Stated in another way directionality in space is the ability to project outside the body the laterality that the child has developed within himself or herself.

The categories of laterality and directionality make up the broader classification of directional awareness. The development of this quality is most important in that it is an essential element in reading and writing. These two basic Rs require the hand and/or eyes to move from the left to the right in a coordinated manner. Also, interpretation of left and right directions is an important requirement for the child in dealing with the environment. It is interesting to note that some children who have not developed laterality quite often will write numbers sequentially from left to right. However, when doing addition and subtraction, they may want to start from left instead of the right. Active play activities designed to differentiate right and left sides of the body are an important part of remedial arithmetic.

Since laterality and directionality are important aspects of body awareness, some of the methods of detecting deficiencies in body awareness mentioned earlier in the chapter also apply here. In addition, it may be noted that the child is inclined to use just the dominant side of the body. Also, confusion may result of the child is given directions for body movements that call for a specific direction in which he or she is to move. In activities that require a child to run to a given point, such as a base, he or she may tend to veer away from it. Or, the child may not perceive the position of other children in the game and, as a consequence may run into them frequently. These are factors that adults can observe in children in their natural play environment, or in their movements about the home.

ACTIVE PLAY EXPERIENCES INVOLVING LATERALITY AND DIRECTIONALITY

Generally speaking, a relatively large number of active play experiences involve some aspects of lateralness, while a more moderate number are concerned with directionality. Some active play experiences involve unilateral movements, those performed with one side or part of the body. Many active play experiences provide for bilateral movement. This means that both sides or segments of the body are in action at the same time in the same manner, as in catching a large ball with both hands. Cross-lateral movement is involved when segments of the body are used at the same time but in a different manner. In fielding a ground ball a child may catch it in one hand and trap it with the other. Many active play experiences are concerned with changing direction, which is likely to involve directionality. The active play experiences that follow have been selected because they contain certain experiences in laterality and/or directionality. Also, in some of the activities, these experiences are more pronounced and receive more emphasis than might be the case with certain other activities.

Zig Zag Run

With the individual child the adult can set up various objects about 4 feet apart and have the child run around them, first to the left and then to the right an so on. This activity gives practice in changing directions as the child runs around the objects. The adult can closely observe how much difficulty is encountered in performing the task. With several players, children can be put into two teams and the activity carried out in relay fashion.

Move Around

The adult and child stand a short distance apart. The adult call out directions in which the child is to move, such as "move to the right," "move forward," and so on. After a time the adult and child change positions and the child becomes the caller.

Catch the Cane

The adult stands a short distance away from the child and with one finger, holds a stick (cane) upright. When the adult calls "Go" the cane is let go and allowed to fall. The child tries to catch the cane before it drops to the surface area. Then the adult and child change places. This activity helps in the development of directionality, eye-hand coordination, and listening discrimination.

Crab Walk

The child sits on the surface area with knees bent and hands on the surface area behind the hips. He or she raises the hips until the trunk is straight. In this position the child walks forward and backward or to the side on hands and feet.

The number of steps taken may be specified with reference to direction; that is, so many steps forward and so many backward. Also, the adult can call out the directions for the "crab" to pursue, forward, backward, or sideward left or right.

Up and Down

The child and adult stand facing each other holding hands. The child stoops down. When he or she stands the adult stoops down. They continue doing so. They can go up and down any number of times, calling out whether they are up or down.

Go and Stop

The activity requires at least three players. They stand around the activity area with one person designated as the leader. The leader points in a given direction and says "Hop that way." Or the leader may say "Skip to the wall." When the leader calls out "Stop," all of the players must stoop down. The idea is not to be the last one down. The last person down has a point scores against him or her and the activity continues for a specified amount of time.

In the early stages of this activity, it is a good idea for the adult to be the leader so he or she can control the various calls. The adult can observe if a child is unable to go immediately in the direction the leader specifies. The adult should be alert to see if a child watches another before making a movement. This can suggest whether a child is having difficulty in following directions.

The Rhythm Game

Creative adults can develop their own rhythmic activities and use movements that they desire. The following original verse, which indicates movements to be made, is an example.

Point to the left.
Now point to the right.
Now turn around with all you might.

Take one step forward.
Take one step back.
Now try to be like a jumping jack.
Point your arms out.
Point your toes in.
Now give yourself a little spin.
Now turn you head.
Now bend your knees.
Now buzz around like a hive of bees.

It is an interesting practice to have the child, with the guidance of the adult also create experiences along the above lines. It has been my experience that activities of this nature are likely to be of extreme value because they are devised to meet the needs of a child or children in a specific situation.

IMPROVING THE FORMS OF PERCEPTION THROUGH ACTIVE PLAY

At the beginning of this chapter, I defined perception as how we obtain information through the senses and what we make of it. I should perhaps mention that this term is often defined differently by different sources. For example, one source might describe perception as an individual's awareness of and reaction to stimuli. Another source might refer to it as the process by which the individual maintains contact with his or her environment. Still another source might describe it as the mental interpretation of messages received through the senses. While there are many descriptions of the term perception, it is likely that the reader will notice that these descriptions are more alike than they are different. My description of perception tends to place the meaning of it in more or less simple terms.

According to the many learning theorists, perception is developmental. That is, it changes with age and experience. Development of perception can occur in three major periods: (1) sensory-motor intelligence, which occurs during the period from birth to about two years, is concerned with learning to coordinate various perceptions and movements; (2) the ages from two to about eleven or twelve involve preparation for and organization of concrete operations, and deal with the acquisition of language (it is during this period that the child learns to deal logically with his or her surroundings); (3) the formal operations that occur after the age of eleven or twelve, and deal with the development of abstract and formal systems.

Learning theorists agree that the forms of perception most involved in learning are auditory perception, visual perception, kinesthetic perception, and tactile perception. These are the topics for discussion in the remainder of this chapter.

Auditory Perception

It has been estimated that about 75 percent of the waking hours are spent in verbal communication – 45 percent in listening, 30 percent in speaking, 16 percent in reading, and the remaining 9 percent in writing. If this estimate is true, the importance of developing skills of listening cannot be denied. If children are going to learn effectively, care should be taken to improve upon their auditory perception – the mental interpretation of what a person hears. Without question, selective attention to sound is essential in helping children increase their effective use of auditory information. Moreover, by becoming a better listener and learning to ignore unrelated noise, the child can begin to hear important concepts needed to improve academic performance.

Active Play Experiences Involving Auditory Perception

Red Rover
The child stands at one end of the activity area, and the adult stands in the middle of the activity area. The area can be about 20 to 30 feet long and about 15 to 20 feet wide. The adult calls "Red Rover, Red Rover let (name of child) come over." The child tries to run to the other end of the playing area before being tagged by the adult. The adult and child change places so that the child can have a turn at being the caller. The child must listen carefully and run at exactly the right time. This activity can be used with several players if desired.

Red Light
The adult and child take positions the same as Red Rover, except that the adult has his or her back to the child. The adult calls out "Green light." At that signal the child starts to run to the other end of the playing area. At any time the adult can call out "Red light," and turn around to face the child. If the child

is caught moving he or she must go back to the starting line. If not, the adult calls "green light" again and the activity continues in this manner. The idea is for the child to get all the way to the goal line on the opposite end of the playing area. The child and adult should change places frequently so that the child can be the caller. The child must listen closely so as not to get caught moving when "Red light" is called.

Clap and Move
The adult claps his or her hands using slow beats or fast beats. The child moves around the area to the sound of the handclaps. The child walks on the slow beat and runs on the fast beat. The child must be alert to respond to the different beats. After a time the adult and child exchange places.

Freeze and Melt
The child moves around the activity area in any way he or she chooses, such as walking, running, or hopping. When the adult calls out "Freeze," the child must stop. When the work "Melt" is called, the child begins to move around again. The child must listen very closely so as not to be caught moving when the word "Freeze" is called. After a time the adult and child can changes places, with the child doing the calling.

Boiling Water
The child stands a short distance away from the adult, holding a rubber ball. When the adult calls "Cold water," the child passes the ball to the adult. If the adult calls "Warm water," the child rolls the ball to the adult. If the adult calls "Boiling water," the child throws the ball into the air. The adult and child should change places frequently so that the child can be the caller. This activity can be used as a diagnostic technique to determine how well the child can distinguish auditory cues and perform the action required.

Dog Chase
This activity requires four or more players. They are divided into two or more groups. The members of each group are given the name of a dog, such as collie, poodle, and so on. The small groups then mingle into one large group. The adult throws a ball or other object away from the groups, at the same time calling one of the dog names. All of the players with this dog name run after the object. The one who gets possession of it first becomes the leader for the next time. The adult can use this activity as a diagnostic technique by

observing if the child who is the "principal" player reacts slowly or does not react at all to the auditory input.

As will be seen later in the book, reading specialists are aware of the importance of auditory perception as one of the early steps in learning to read. It is suggested by some that the ability to discriminate sounds auditorily is not only an advantage in speech but probably gives an important boost in reading ability. It has been found that active play experiences can provide an important part in the aspect of auditory perception that is concerned with auditory discrimination.

Visual Perception

Visual perception can be defined as the mental interpretation of what a person sees. A number of aspects of visual perception have been identified, and children who have a deficiency in any of these may have difficulty in school performance.

As mentioned in the previous chapter, various estimates indicate that the visual sense brings us upwards of three-fourths of our knowledge. If this is true, then certainly important consideration should be give to how well active play experiences can contribute to visual perception.

Active Play Experiences Involving Visual Perception

The activities that follow are primarily concerned with visualization and visual-motor coordination. Visualization involves visual image, which is the mental reconstruction of visual experience, or the result of mentally combining a number of visual experiences. Visual-motor coordination is concerned with visual-motor tasks that involve the working together of vision and movement.

Hit the Balloon

The child is given a big balloon, and he or she tries to hit it as many times as possible with the hand before the balloon touches the ground. Other things that the child can do with the balloon are to hit it off a wall or hit the balloon back and forth with the adult. This activity is good for eye-hand-coordination.

Big Ball, Little Ball

The adult and child sit on the floor about 10 feet from each other. One has a large ball such as a beach ball and the other a smaller ball. The adult gives a signal, and the big ball is rolled and the small ball is thrown. Both the adult and the child try to catch the ball, and the activity continues in this manner.

Peas Porridge

The child and adult stand facing each other. They slap knees, clap their own hands and each other's hands while they say "Peas porridge hot, peas porridge cold. Peas porridge in the pot. Nine days old!"

Policeman

The adult is the policeman and stands a given distance away from the child. The adult (policeman) carries a card, red on one side and green on the other. At the signal to go (green) from the adult the child sees how far he or she can go before the stop signal (red) is given. If the child moves after the stop signal is given, he or she must go back to the original starting point. The adult and child can change places frequently.

Rather than using the colors, the words Stop and Go can be used on the card so that the child can become familiar with the words as well as the colors. This activity helps the child coordinate movement with the visual experience. It can also help the child become more adept at visual-motor association. The adult should be alert to observe if the child does not stop on signal.

Keep It Up

Depending on the ability level of the child, a large rubber ball, a beach ball, or a large balloon can be use for this activity. On a signal the child tosses the ball into the air, and together the adult and child see how long they can keep it up without its touching the surface area. This is a good activity for the improvement of eye-hand coordination.

Ball Handling Activities

Various kind of ball-handling activities provide outstanding experiences for eye-hand coordination. The activities that follow can be used for this purpose and are a great deal of fun to try. The type of ball used should be one that is suited to the ability of the child.

1. Stationary Bounce. Using both hands, the child bounces the ball to the surface area and catches it while standing in place. This can be repeated any number of times.
2. Walking Bounce. Using both hands, the child bounces the ball to the surface area and catches it while walking.
3. Partner Bounce. Using both hands, the child bounces the ball to the adult, who returns it. The distance between the adult and the child can be increased as desired.
4. Stationary Tap. The child taps the ball with one hand while standing in place. Either hand can be used, depend upon the individual child, and the tapping can be repeated any number of times. (In bouncing, the child gains control of the ball each time; in tapping the child keeps it going for a given number of times without gaining control of the ball.)
5. Walking Tap. The child taps the ball with either hand while walking along. This can be done any number of times.
6. Bounce-Clap-Catch. The child bounces the ball to the surface area and claps the hands before catching it.
7. Bounce-Turn-Catch. The child bounces the ball and turns around to catch it before it bounces a second time. At the onset of this activity it may be a good idea for the child to throw the ball into the air and then turn around and catch it on the bounce. In this variation the child has more time to turn around before the ball bounces.
8. Leg-Over-Bounce. The child bounces the ball, swings a leg over it, and catches it. This can be done with either leg, and then legs can be alternated.
9. Leg-Over-Tap. This is the same as the Leg-Over-Bounce except that the child causes the ball to bounce by continuous tapping.

Kinesthetic Perception

Kinesthesis, the kinesthetic sense, has been described in many ways. Some descriptions of the term are somewhat comprehensive, while others are less so. One comprehensive description of kinesthesis is that it is the sense which enables us to determine the position of the segments of the body, their rate, extent, and direction of movement, the position of the entire body, and the characteristics of total body motion. Another, less complicated description of the term characterizes it as the sense that tells the individual where his or her body is and how it moves.

In summarizing the many descriptions of the term, the following four factors seem to be constant, thus emphasizing the likeliness of the many descriptions of the term: (1) position of the body segments, (2) precision of movement, (3) balance, and (4) space orientation. For discussion here I will think of kinesthetic perception as the mental interpretation of the sensation of body movement.

Although there are a number of specific test items that are supposed to measure kinesthesis, the use of such tests may be of questionable value in diagnosing deficiencies in young children. Therefore, my recommendation is that adults resort to the observation of certain behaviors and mannerisms of children, using simple diagnostic techniques to determine deficiencies in kinesthetic sensitivity.

Children with kinesthetic problems possess characteristics that may be identifying factors. I have found in some cases that a child who is deficient in kinesthetic sensitivity will likely be clumsy, awkward, and inefficient in his or her movements and impaired in getting acquainted with and handling the world of objects. A child who has difficulty in the use of the hands or body in attempting to perform unfamiliar tasks involving body movement can no doubt benefit from activities involving kinesthesis.

With reference to the above, the adult should be on the alert to observe a child who has difficulty with motor-coordination; that is, using the muscles in such a manner that they work together effectively. Such lack of coordination may be seen in children who have difficulty in performing the movement skills that involve uneven rhythm, such as skipping. Adults can observe these deficiencies in the natural play activities of children, and a skill such as skipping can be used as a diagnostic technique in identifying such problems. (Skipping starts with a step and a hop on the same foot and can be taught from the walk. The push-off should be such a forceful upward one that the foot leaves the surface area. To maintain balance, a hop is taken. The sequence is step, push-off high, and hop. The hop occurs on the same foot that was pushing off, and this is the skip. Some children will perform a variation of the skip around four years of age. With proper instruction, a majority of children should be able to accomplish this skill by age six.)

Since balance is an important aspect of kinesthesis, simple tests for balance can be administered to determine if there is a lack of proficiency. One such test would be to have the child stand on either food. Ordinarily, a child should be able to maintain such a position for a period of at least five seconds.

Active Play Experiences Involving Kinesthetic Perception
     Since kinesthetic sensitivity is concerned with the sensation of movement and orientation of the body in space, it is not an easy matter to isolate specific active play experiences suited only for this purpose. The reason for this is that practically all-active play experiences involve total or near total physical response. Therefore, practically all-active play experiences are of value in the improvement of kinesthetic sensitivity. However, the kinds of active play experiences that make the child particularly aware of the movement of certain muscle groups, as well as those where he or she encounters resistance, are of particular value in helping the child develop kinesthetic awareness of the body.

Poison
     This activity requires several players. The players form a circle and join hands. A circle is drawn on the activity area inside the circle of players and about 12 to 18 inches in front of the feet of the circle of players. With hands joined, they pull and tug each other, trying to make one or more of the players step into the drawn circle. Anyone who steps into the circle is said to be "poisoned." As soon as a person is poisoned, someone calls out "Poison!" and the one who is poisoned becomes It and give chase to the others. The other players run to various objects of certain material previously designated as safety, such as wood, stone, or metal. All of the players tagged are poisoned and become chasers. After those not tagged have reached safety, the leader calls out "Change!" and they must run to another safety point. Those tagged attempt to tag as many others as possible. The activity can continue until all but one have been poisoned.
     This activity provides an opportunity for kinesthetic awareness as a child tries to keep from being pulled into the circle. Also, surface area resistance may be encountered depending upon the type of surface where the activity takes place.

We Swing
     This is a rhythmic activity and as such is concerned with body movement and the position of the body in space. It is the type of rhythmic activity that can make a child aware of the movement of certain muscle groups. The

activity is in song-story form, and the adult and child together can make up a tune to it if they wish. Creative adults along with children should be able to make up some of these kinds of activities on their own.

> We hold hands (adult and child hold hands standing side by side)
> We will try to swing.
> We swing our arms (adult and child swing both arms).
> We swing.
> We swing.
> We take four steps in (adult and child run four steps forward).
> We take four steps out (adult and child walk back four steps).
> We drop our hands.
> We turn about.

Ball-Handling Activities

The ball-handling activities that were previously explained, when used with different sized balls, are of value as far as timing relates to kinesthetic perception. These activities are recommended for this purpose.

Tactile Perception

The tactile sense is very closely related to the kinesthetic sense, so much so in fact that these two senses are often confused. One of the reasons for this is that the ability to detect changes in touch (tactile) involves many of the same receptors concerned with informing the body of changes in its position. The essential difference between the tactile sense and the kinesthetic sense may be seen in the descriptions of kinesthetic and tactile perception. As stated previously kinesthetic perception involves the mental interpretation of the sensation of movement, whereas tactile perception is concerned with the mental interpretation of what a person experiences through the sense of touch.

Since the kinesthetic and tactile senses are so closely related, the identifying factors of deficiency in kinesthesis previously reported can also be used to determine if there is a deficiency in the tactile sense. Also a number of elementary diagnostic techniques for tactile sensitivity can be played in a game type of situation so that the child is unaware of being tested. The following list suggests some representative examples, and creative adults are limited only by their own imagination in expanding the list.

1. Have the child explore the surface and texture of objects around the home. Determine if he or she can differentiate among these objects.
2. Evaluate the child's experience by having him or her give the names of two or three hard objects, two or three rough objects, and so on.
3. Make a touching box by using an ordinary shoebox. Place differently shaped objects and differently textured objects in the box. Have the child reach into the box without looking, and have him or her feel the various objects to see if he or she can identify them.

Active Play Experiences Involving Tactile Perception

Children need tactile stimulation through touching and being touched. The following active play experiences, which involve touching and being touched, apply not only to tactile stimulation but also to tactile communication as a means of social interaction referred to previously.

Touch Something

In this activity the child runs around the activity area and touches differently textured objects called out by the adult. For example, the adult can say "Touch something hard," "Touch something rough," etc. The idea is to see how quickly the child can react and make the touch on the correct object. After a time the child should be given the opportunity to be the caller.

Electric Shock

This activity requires about five or more players, who form a circle with one player designated to be It. The player who is It stands inside the circle and attempts to determine where the electric power is concentrated. The players in the circle join hands and one player is designated to start the electricity. This player accomplishes this by tightly squeezing the hand of the player on either side. As soon as a person's hand is squeezed, he or she keeps the electricity moving by squeezing the hand of the next person. If It knows where the electric power is, that is, whose hand is being squeezed, he or she calls out that person's name. If It guessed correctly, all of the players in the circle run to a previously designated safety area to avoid being tagged by It. If desired, a point can be scored against all of those tagged, and the activity continues with another player becoming It. In this situation, the tactile sense becomes a medium of communication as each child's hand is squeezed by another.

Cat and Mouse

This activity requires several players, at least six or more. One child is chosen to be the mouse and another child is the cat. The remaining players join hands and form a circle, with the mouse in the center of the circle and the cat on the outside of the circle. The players in the circle try to keep the cat from getting into the circle and catching the mouse. If the cat gets inside the circle, the players in the circle let the mouse outside of the circle and try to keep the cat in, but they must keep their hands joined at all times. If the cat catches the mouse the activity is over, and those players join the circle while two others become the cat and mouse. If the mouse is not caught in a specified period of time, a new cat and mouse can be selected.

The players can see the importance of working together with joined hands. When the cat tries to enter the circle at a given point between two players, those players can feel the tight grip of the hands needed to protect the mouse.

Stunt Play

Certain stunts provide fine possibilities for tactile perception in that some of them afford opportunities for body contact with others as well as with the surface area. Some representative examples of these kinds of activities follow.

1. Seal Crawl. The child supports himself or herself on the hands while the body is extended back. The child squats and places the hands on the surface area shoulder width apart, palms flat, and fingers pointed forward. He or she extends the legs in the back until the body is straight. The child points the toes so that a part of the weight will be on the top of the feet. The child is now ready to move forward on the hands, dragging the feet.

2. Churn the Butter. This activity involves two children about the same size. They turn back-to-back and lock elbows by bending their arms to approximately a 90-degree angle. The elbows are held in back of each performer, and the forearms are held against the ribs. One child picks up the other child from the surface area by bending forward with a slow, controlled movement. The other child will momentarily have the feet slightly off the surface area. The first child releases the lifting force by straightening to an erect standing position; the other child then lifts the first child in the same manner. This action is repeated as long as desired.

3.   Wheelbarrow. A child has a partner of about equal size and strength. One of the pair assumes a position with the hands on the surface area, with elbows straight, and feet extended behind. The other child carries the feet of the first child, who keeps his or her knees straight. This child becomes the wheelbarrow by walking on the hands. Positions are changed so that each can become the wheelbarrow.

All of the active play experiences in this chapter have been field tested, and when presented properly have met with various degrees of success.

Chapter 7

ALL ABOUT READING

It has been suggested that the ability to read was not considered important for most laymen until sometime after Johann Gutenberg invented the printing press in the 15th century, and the Protestant Reformation with its emphasis on individual interpretation of the Bible. Until that time, reading was generally restricted to the clergy and certain members of the nobility. [1]

THE NATURE OF READING

Practically all of us learn to read but, of course, with varying degrees of proficiency. Yet, to define exactly what reading means is not an easy task. A part of the reason for this is that it means different things to different people. The psychologist thinks of reading as a thought process. Those who deal with semantics, which is the study of meanings, think of reading as the graphic representation of speech. The linguist, one who specializes in speech and language, is concerned with the sounds of language and its written form. Finally, the sociologist is concerned with the interaction of reading and culture.

Reading is an aspect of communication, and as such it becomes more than just being able to recognize a word on a printed page. To communicate, a meaning must be shared and the reader must be able to comprehend. Thus, one of the most important concerns in teaching reading is that of helping children develop comprehension skills.

Reading could be thought of as bringing meaning to the printed page as well as gaining meaning from it. This means that the author of a reading selection does not necessarily convey ideas to the reader but simulates him or her to construct them out of his or her own experience. (This is one of the major purposes of active play reading content which will be dealt with in a later chapter.)

Since reading is such a complex act and cannot be easily defined, I will resort to a rather broad and comprehensive description of the term. My description of reading is an interpretation of written or printed verbal symbols. This can range from graffiti on restroom walls to the Harvard Classics.

It should be borne in mind that the entire child reads. He or she reads with the senses, past experiences, cultural heritage, and of course with the muscles. It is the latter aspect with which I am predominantly concerned, because the aspect of "muscle sense" involved in active play is an extremely important dimension in reading for children.

EYE MOVEMENTS IN READING

Early studies in reading focused on the visual act of reading as a means of better understanding the process. Extensive research in this area continued through the 1940s. Such research resulted in the development of reading-eye cameras such as the Ophthalmograph (American Optical Company) by which eye movements could be recorded and analyzed.

From these studies the pattern of eye movements in the reading act is one of the eyes moving from left to right across the line of print with a return sweep to the next line, proceeding in a left-to-right direction again. This rhythmic movement line after line is broken by fixations as the eyes move across the line and regressions or backward movements.

At fixation points the eyes are not in motion. It is at this moment, however, that the vision is not blurred by movement and the visual act of reading takes place. The time of "fixation" may vary from a third to a fourth of a second and is affected by the skill development of the reader and the difficulty of the material. Approximately 90 percent of the time spent in reading is accounted for by fixation points when the reader is going through the "seeing," the word-recognition, and the association process.

Regressions occur when there is a breakdown in the word-recognition or comprehension of the idea being presented. Some reading specialists caution that an excessive proportion of unknown words, inadequate experiences with the multiple meanings of words, and reading matter which is much too complex for the child's experiences all promote a faulty reading pattern and lack of progress in reading.

Eye span is another term used in describing the visual act. Eye span is the span of recognition during the moment of "fixation." For the elementary school child the eye span may be limited to the point where there is an average of two fixation points per word. The limitations of the eye span also indicates the demand upon the eyes in terms of the number of times the eyes converge in perfect alignment to focus on each "fixation."

As a visual task, adequate vision for reading calls for coordination and motility with accurate binocular shifts from point to point, accurate focus and accommodation to distance, a fine degree of parallel or coordinated action of both eyes and left-to-right directional attack.

When there is difficulty of function in eye movements this can result in loss of place, omissions, excessive repetitions, and slow rate. Defects in coordination, motility, directional attack, and form perception can prevent development of a desirable pattern of eye movement.

When there is evidence of deficiencies in visual perception or eye-hand coordination, developmentally training can be given. Three major types of visual training for perception and discrimination are (1) directionality, or orientation to direction, (2) ocular motility, or promoting coordinated movements of both eyes , and (3) form perception, or discrimination of similarities and differences in designs, figures, and word-like forms. (Some examples of how this training can be accomplished were presented in the preceding chapter.)

WHEN TO BEGIN READING INSTRUCTION

Traditionally, the standard practice has been to begin the teaching of reading when children enter first grade at school at about six years of age. However, in modern times there appears to be a great deal of sentiment to start reading instruction before that time. A part of the reason for this is that there is a general feeling that young children are becoming more mature and possess greater experience at an earlier age than was the case in the past. As a result of this prevailing belief, fully one-third of the teachers at the kindergarten level feel that their children can benefit from various forms of reading instruction. In fact, a large majority of kindergarten teachers conduct some of the fundamental phases of reading instruction and only about 20 percent of them do not believe that reading instruction should be a part of the school program at that level.

A question that must be raised is: Does early reading instruction have any value? Completely solid evidence to support one position or another is lacking to make an unqualified valid conclusion. One very important consideration is whether or not early instruction benefits the child as far as his or her total development is concerned. Some child development specialists feel that such instruction, if too highly structured and formalized can actually cause harm to some children as far as their emotional development and social adjustment are concerned.

It is important to mention again at this point that education is as much the business of the home as of the school, because it is obvious that the school alone does not educate the child. Yet, many parents believe that a child begins to learn only when he or she enters a school. They do not seem to realize that they are not only the child's first teacher but probably the most important one the child will ever have.

Parents can and should help prepare their children before they enter school and also assist their children with their schoolwork after they are in school. An abundance of evidence is being accumulated to support this idea. For example, I have found in my surveys that preschool children who have been "read to" by their parents or others perform better than those who do not receive such attention.

There are many valid reasons why this is true. Research in child development indicates that the direction of a child's mental development is likely to be determined between ten months and one and one-half years of age – and in some cases even lower. In addition, the human learning patterns can become well established by age three. Consequently, the action that parents take in helping their children is extremely important. Moreover, most authorities in the area of child development tend to feel that the first five years are the most important formative ones in a child's life. The child's ability to learn various skills in these formative years before he or she enters school may depend a good bit on the extent to which parents provide him or her with desirable and worthwhile learning experiences.

Of the millions of children entering first grade about ten percent of them will be asked to repeat that grade. If the present trends continue, one-fourth of first grade children, by the time they reach the age of eleven, will be reading two or more years below grade level.

It is easy to blame the schools for this sad state of affairs. However, before doing so we might well take another look at the responsibility of parents as important helpers in the education of their children.

READING READINESS

Closely allied to the problem of when to begin reading instruction is the question of reading readiness. There are certain developmental tasks that are important for children to accomplish. Reading can be considered as such a developmental task. That is, it is a task that a child needs to perform to satisfy his or her personal needs as well as those requirements which society and the culture impose upon children. In viewing reading as a developmental task, we can then consider reading readiness as a developmental stage at which certain factors have prepared the child for reading.

At one time, reading readiness was considered only as being with the child being ready to begin the reading experience. In modern times it has become to be thought of more in term of each step of reading as one concerned with readiness for further reading. Therefore, the idea of reading readiness is not confined only to the start of reading instruction but to the teaching the learning of most all reading skills. A given child may be considered ready to learn to read at a certain age. However, this same child may not necessarily be ready to read to learn until a later time. In fact, some reading specialist consider the primary level of grades one through three as a time for learning to read, and the intermediate level of grades four through six as a time when the child begins to read to learn.

Reading readiness needs to be thought of as a complex combination of basic abilities and conditions and not only as a single characteristic. This combination of (1) various aspects includes visual ability, (2) certain factors concerned with the auditory sense, (3) sex differences, (4) age, and (5) socioeconomic conditions. Obviously, it not my purpose here to go into detail with reference to these various characteristics but merely to identify them at this point. In the following chapter some specific recommendations will be made concerning the application and function of active play as a medium for dealing with certain aspect of reading readiness.

SCHOOL READING PROGRAMS

One of the very important school curriculum areas in the education of young children is the language arts program. This program includes listening, speaking, reading, and writing, all of which are concerned with communication. The primary purpose of the language arts program in the modern elementary school is to facilitate communication.

Speaking and writing can be referred to as the expressive phases of language, while listening and reading are considered the receptive phases. This implies that through speaking and writing the individual has the opportunity to express his or her own thoughts and feelings to others. Through reading and listening the individual receives the thoughts and feelings of others.

Although I have indicated that the language arts program contains listening, speaking, reading, and writing, the reader should not interpret this to mean that these are considered as entirely separate entities. On the contrary, they are closely interrelated, and each can be considered a component part of the broad area of communication. Such areas of study in the school as spelling, word meanings, and word recognition are involved in each of the four areas.

The importance of the interrelationship of the various language arts can be shown in different ways. For example, children must use words that they read with understanding and that they want to use for their own purposes. In addition, their handwriting even improves when they use it in a purposeful and meaningful way of communication when someone they like is going to read it. Perhaps the two most closely interrelated and interdependent phases of the language arts are listening and reading. In fact, most reading specialists agree that learning to listen is the first step in learning to read. This relationship will be very apparent, particularly in Chapter 10 of the book.

The modern elementary school gives a great deal of attention to this interrelationship of the various phases of the language arts. This is reflected in the way in which language experiences are being provided in the better-than-average elementary school. In the traditional elementary school it was a common practice to treat such aspects of the language arts as reading, writing and spelling as separate subjects. As a result, they became more or less isolated and unrelated entities, and their full potential as media of expression probably was never fully realized. In the modern elementary school, where children have more freedom of expression and, consequently, greater opportunity for self-expression, the approach to teaching language arts is one that relates the various language areas to particular areas of interest. All of the phases of language arts – listen, speaking, reading, and writing – are thus used in the solution of problems in all curriculum areas. This procedure is primarily based upon the assumption that skill in communication should be developed in all of the activities engaged in by children.

I have already said that through reading the individual receives the thoughts and feelings of others; therefore, reading is considered a receptive phase of language. In this case the word receptive might well carry a figurative as well as purely literal meaning. Indeed, reading has been on the "receiving end" of a great deal of criticism over the years. Perhaps more criticism has been directed at it than all of the other school subjects combined. Although it may be difficult to determine precisely why reading has suffered the brunt of attack, one could speculate that it might be because, in general, many people consider reading as the real test of learning. In fact, in the early days of American education, grade levels tended to be thought of as "readers;" that is, a child was said to be in the "first reader," "second reader," and so one.

In modern times a good bit of the controversy involving reading seems to center around two general areas. First, there has been criticism of the various methods of teaching reading, and second, there has been some question regarding the validity of the principles upon which these methods are based. Perhaps because of the individual differences, any method used in absolute form to the exclusion of all other methods would not meet the needs of all children. For this reason it seems logical to assume that the procedure or combination of procedures employed should be those which best meets the needs of an individual child or a particular group of children.

It is not my purpose here to extol or criticize any of the past or present methods of teaching reading. Rather, my recommendation is intended to show how active play experiences can be used to assist the child in his or her efforts to read.

Whenever innovations in instruction are recommended there is always concern that these innovations are consistent with what is now known about child growth and development as well as principles of learning. This is rightly so. As these innovations are being tried, there must also be an evaluation of their effectiveness in terms of education objectives. The following three chapters will therefore focus upon the theoretical basis of the physical aspect of the total personality and learning to read, along with specific use of the active play learning medium in such areas of reading as teaching children to read, diagnosing readiness and reading ability, teaching reading skills, and active play reading content.

Despite recurring admonitions as to the dangers of trying the "new" simply to be able to be identified as having innovative and progressive programs, there pervades throughout the literature a sense of urgency for new approaches and materials, different and more effective uses of the old approaches and materials, adaptive combinations of the old and new – something different, something that will work better than what our current reading instruction programs are producing. Programs are looking for answers from both the old and the innovative. But the message of the program is that we must try and we must find answers.

NOTE

[1] *The New Columbia Encyclopedia*, New York, Columbia University Press, 4th ed., 1975, p. 2284.

Chapter 8

DIAGNOSIS OF READING READINESS THROUGH ACTIVE PLAY

A standard general description of the term diagnosis is the act of identifying a condition from its signs and symptoms. Applied to reading, diagnosis implies an analysis of reading behavior for purposes of discovering strengths and weaknesses of a child as a basis for more effective guidance of his or her reading efforts.

Among other things, it is important to try to discover why a child reads as he or she does, what a child is able to read and what is read successfully. In addition, we need to know if the child is having problems in reading, what these problems are, and the causes of the problems.

In the school situation many diagnostic tests are available for use and they have various degrees of validity. Studies tend to show that teachers themselves can forecast reading success of first grade children with about as much accuracy as reading readiness tests. It may be that such success in teacher observation has been a part of the reason for what is called diagnostic teaching becoming so important as school systems address their attention to meeting the needs of individual children.

DIAGNOSIS IN THE SCHOOL CLASSROOM

Over the years the term diagnosis has generally been thought of as a more formal out-of-classroom procedure for those children the teacher identifies as having difficulties in their attempts to learn to read. Occasionally, diagnosis is requested for those children whom teachers consider as not working up to their potential. More and more reading specialists are recognizing that information about the reading skill strengths and needs of children to help the classroom teacher make appropriate adjustments in instruction. Such adjustments involve focus on specific skills, level of material, and method of instruction.

Classroom diagnosis has been directed to assessing the skills strengths and needs of children, either prior to or after instruction. Traditional measures have been standardized tests (usually of a survey nature), informal inventories, or teacher-made tests. The value of teacher observations of children during different types of reading situations has been recognized as essential to supplement information received from the traditional measures. Such observations are likely to be followed by recording and analyzing their reading performance.

The procedure of observing, recording, and analyzing a child's performance during the learning activity has come to be recognized as perhaps a more reliable assessment of his or her skills development. Such procedures have become the framework for diagnostic teaching. Diagnostic teaching is concerned with an understanding of the reading strengths and needs of each child. These understandings should be used to modify instructional methods so that teaching, adjusted to the changing needs of the children, can be maintained. Such teaching is based on continuous diagnosis of the skill development of each child.

One of the many problems inherent in testing situations is the effect of a child's apprehension on his or her performance of the task involved. Basic principles of clinical diagnosis in reading have alluded to this problem by emphasizing the important of establishing rapport with the child, starting the testing with less-threatening types of tasks, and stopping at the frustration level before complete discouragement disintegrates the testing situation. Teachers using such classroom diagnosis measures as mentioned often voice a concern relating to this apprehension on the part of children. They realize the child must be put at ease as to the nature and reason for testing. Paper-and-pencil tests throughout the grades, along with the aptitude tests and college entrance examinations, have resulted in adult aversion to test-taking to the point of significant blocking of what might be a usual performance level of an individual when not under stress.

Diagnostic Teaching Techniques

Diagnostic teaching techniques employing observation, recording, and analysis of children's performance in day-to-day reading situations has become a significant trend in assessment. Obtaining daily feedback is a key to structuring appropriate day-to-day learning activities, because they are based on the "real" reading performance of the child. It is a better "reading" of where the child is in his or her skills development. Therefore, in diagnostic teaching, we are using such techniques as coding errors made by children while oral reading to prove points in the discussion of material they are reading for a directed reading-thinking activity. In this way, we gain information about the children's sight vocabulary, word-attack application to unfamiliar words in context reading, and comprehension skills.

The every-pupil-response technique is used as a diagnostic teaching procedure in many types of situations. With the technique calling for each child in a group to respond to a question or problem by holding up an answer card or signaling with a finger response a choice of answers, we are able to check the performance of all the children. We can observe each child's understanding and interpreting of the material, and his or her application of a specific skill to new words as in the case of reading. This technique not only provides information about each child's skills development within a group activity, but it also involves each child consistently throughout the learning and application of skills. This aspect of maximum involvement of each child within a group activity is particularly inherent in active play experiences. An example of this is the game "Match Cats," which is described later in this chapter.

It is interesting to note that these diagnostic techniques are geared to observing an individual child's performance within group learning activities. Teachers employing these techniques have reported they are better able to plan further activities for children to meet their individual needs through sub-grouping children for additional learning experiences. As a result, the individualizing of instruction, a major objective of the schools becomes a reality.

ACTIVE PLAY AS A DIAGNOSTIC TEACHING TECHNIQUE

By using active play experiences the use of children's naturally physically oriented world becomes a positive factor operating to facilitate further interest as well as more involvement and attending to the learning task. Many children tend to lose their apprehension to the learning task when it is "buried" in the context of an active play experience.

In particular, disabled readers will often perform tasks such as auditory and visual discrimination while engaging in an active play experience like "Man from Mars," "Match Cards," and "Letter Spot" when they might be saying "I can't do it" in more traditional learning activities. (Descriptions of these activities are presented later in the chapter.) Observations of children with severe reading problems, whose discouragement and frustration initially hampers their willingness even to participate, have found their natural affinity for physical activity has been the starting point of a more accurate assessment of their skill strengths and needs as well as remediation.

The total physical involvement of such children through active play experiences related to reading appears to act as a means for releasing the emotional blockage that inhibits any attempts to perform the intellectual reading tasks involved. And once these children participate successfully in such activities because of the strengthening of input through active play, the process of building more positive attitudes toward reading and a feeling that they can learn is begun. Needless to say, once the teacher has observed a higher-level performance of children in this setting, it is important to help the children recognize that they were able to, and did, perform the skill involved. Such children need to be shown they can and have mastered a skill with specific evidence that they have learned.

Four important factors in the active play experiences that the teacher can utilize to determine whether further learning experiences are necessary for skill mastery are (1) the type of sensory input or modality involved in the reading task inherent in the active play experience, (2) the accuracy of the child's responses in the reading task, (3) the reaction time of children in performing that reading task, and (4) the self-evaluation of the child of his or her performance.

Sound instructional programs have always been specific-skill oriented. The impact of establishing behaviorally stated goals as objectives for instruction has helped teachers to move beyond such lesson plan goals as "learning word-attack skills" to "being able to identify by name the initial letter of a word given orally" or "being able to give orally another word that begins with the same sound as a word presented visually." In the latter lesson objectives, both input and output modality are clearly stated so that a teacher observing such activities can analyze children's performance in regard to sensory modality both for input and output production. Such information helps the teacher to identify those children who consistently give evidence of significant differences in performance when lesson input is basically auditory or visual. Such information helps the teacher to adapt instruction accordingly and thereby assure more meaningful, and more successful, learning-to-read experiences.

Active play experiences related to reading by their very nature enables the teacher to identify the specific reading skills involved. The reading skills utilized in active play can be readily identified. An example of this would be the activity "Letter Spot" in which the reading skill is one of visual recognition of upper and lower case letters in order to play the activity. (This activity is explained later in the chapter.)

The second factor in the active play experience which a teacher can utilize is the accuracy of children's responses to the reading task inherent in the activity. It can be observed in those children who use the specific skill with at least 90 percent accuracy in their responses. This should represent skill mastery at the independent level. Any lower percentage of accuracy would indicate additional experiences are necessary.

The third factor relating to the reaction time of children's performance during active play experience helps the teacher to identify the ease and comfort of children in performing a specific task. Reaction time in the present context refers to the amount of time it takes for the onset of a response of a person after receiving a stimulus. By observing the quickness of a child's response to the reading task inherent in the active play experience the teacher can assess the degree of ease as well as the accuracy of the child's responses. While percentage of accuracy is a useful and necessary tool in determining when a child reaches the point of skill mastery, the ease and comfort of the child during the reading task is also significant. Skill mastery implies operation of an "automatic" level independently.

Of particular concern in consideration of reaction time are those children who have a disability in processing the sensory input with a resulting delay in reaction to the question or task presented. Such impairment can affect auditory, visual or feeling input. This may be related to the first factor in the use of active play as a diagnostic tool in which the teacher is observing children's performance in terms of modality used. In the activity "Call and Catch" (described later), the teacher adjusts the timing by momentarily holding the ball before throwing it into the air. In the case of reaction time there may simply be a lesser degree of impairment resulting only in more reaction time necessary to perform the task. The teacher must be aware that children may have this type of disability and attempt to recognize those children who consistently need additional time to respond to the task. It is important to adjust to the needs of such children rather than categorizing their delay in responding as being the result of categorizing their delay in responding as being the result of disinterest or uncooperativeness. Active play experiences can easily be adapted to such children.

The fourth factor is that of self-evaluation by the children themselves. Children should be encouraged not only to react to the activity itself but also to assess how they did and what they might do to improve their performance of the reading skill involved. It might be a case of looking more carefully at the word, picture, or design card used in the active play experience. In such pleasurable activities children appear more willing to examine their performance in the learning tasks involved, and quite realistically as well.

The uniqueness of active play, therefore, as another means of diagnosis, is that such experiences tend to remove the apprehension of testing procedures and can demonstrate a level of skills development that is possibly more consistent with day-to-day performance. Such performance of the reading skill involved in the active play experience might even appear higher than when the children are engaged in more traditional reading activities. This higher level performance should then be taken as a more accurate assessment of children's potential level of performance when they are operating under optimum conditions of learning.

DIAGNOSING READING READINESS
SKILLS THROUGH ACTIVE PLAY

Reading readiness skills are a complex cluster of basic skills, including (1) language development in which the child learns to transform his or her experience and his or her environment into language symbols through listening, oral language facility and meaningful vocabulary; (2) the skills relating to the mechanics of reading such as left-to-right orientation, auditory and visual discrimination, and recognition of letter names and sounds; and (3) the cognitive processes of comparing, classifying, ordering, interpreting, summarizing, and imagining.

Likewise, sensory-motor skills provide a foundation for these basic skills by sharpening the senses and developing motor skills involving spatial, form, and time concepts. The following list identifies some concepts developed through direct body movement.

1. Body Awareness
2. Space and Direction
3. Balance
4. Basic Body Movements
5. Eye-Hand Coordination
6. Eye-Foot Coordination
7. Form Perception
8. Rhythm
9. Large Muscle Activity
10. Fine Muscle Activity

These skills are essential to the establishment of a sound foundation for the beginning-to-read experiences of children. Not only can the reading readiness program, structured for the development of these skills, be facilitated through active play experiences, but diagnosis of progress in skills development can be obtained by teacher observation and children's self-evaluation. Active play experiences can be utilized effectively to provide meaningful and satisfying learning activities in the reading readiness program. The following active play experiences are described to indicate the variety of activities that may be employed in the development and assessment of reading skills.

Language Development

In such activities as the following, concept formation is translated into meaningful vocabulary.

Concept: Classification

Activity: Pet Store
One fairly large Pet Store is marked off at one end of the activity area and a Home at the other end. At the side of is a Cage. In the center of the playing area stands the Pet Store Owner. All of the players stand in the Pet Store and are given a picture of one kind of pet (for example, fish, bird, dog). There should be about two or three pictures of each kinds of pet. The Pet Store Owner calls "Fish" (or any of the other pets in the activity). The players who have pictures of fish must try to run from the Pet Store to their new Home without being caught or tagged by the Owner. If they are caught, they must go to the Cage and wait for the next call. The activity continues until all the Pets have tried to get to their new Home. Kinds of pets can changed frequently.

Application: By grouping themselves according to the animal pictures, children are able to practice classifying things that swim , things that fly, and so forth. At the end of the activity they can count how many fish, dogs, and so forth were caught. All the fish, birds, dogs, and so forth can then form their own line to swim, fly, or walk back to the Pet Store, where new pictures can be given to the children for another game.

Concept: Vocabulary Meaning – Action Words

Activity: What to Play
One child is selected as the leader. The others sing:

> Mary tell us what to play,
> What to play, what to play,
> Mary tell us what to play,
> Tell us what to play.

(The song is sung to the tune of "Mary Had a Little Lamb.") The leader then says, "Let's play we're fish," or "Let's wash dishes." Or "Let's throw a ball."
The leader then performs some action that the other players have to imitate. One a signal, the players stop and a new leader is selected.
Application: This activity gives children an opportunity to act out meanings of words. It helps them to recognize that spoken words represent actions of people as well as things that can be touched.

Concept: Vocabulary Meaning – Left and Right

Activity: Changing Seats

Enough chairs for each player in the group are placed side by side in about four or five rows. The players sit alert, ready to move either way. The leader calls, "Change right!" and each player moves to the seat too his or her right. When the leader calls, "Change left!" each player moves left. The player at the end of the row who does not have a seat to move to must run to the other end of the row to sit in the vacant seat there. The leader can bring excitement to the activity by calling the same direction several times in succession. After each command the first row of players who all find seats may score a point for that row.

Application: This type of activity makes children more aware of the necessity of differentiating left from right. At the beginning of the activity, children may not be able to differentiate directions rapidly. The teacher will need to gear the rapidity of his or her commands according to the skills of the group.

Auditory Discrimination

The following activity shows not only an active play experience using auditory discrimination skills be also the way activities can be adapted to other reading skills.

Concept: Auditory Discrimination – Beginning Sound of Words

Activity: Man from Mars

One child is selected to be the Man from Mars and stands in the center of the activity area. The other players stand behind a designated line at one end of the area. The activity begins when the players call out, "Man from Mars, can we chase him through the stars?" The leader answers, "Yes, if your name begins like duck" (or any other word). All the players whose name begins with the same beginning sound as duck, or whatever word is called, chase the Man from Mars until he is caught. The player who tags him becomes the new Man from Mars and the activity continues.

Application: In order for the players to run at the right time, they must listen carefully and match beginning sounds. If the teacher sees a child not running when he or she should, individual help can be given. Children can also listen for words beginning like or ending like other words the teacher may use for the key word.

Visual Discrimination

The various activities described here relating to visual discrimination indicate the variety of active play situations which can be utilized to develop skills or to assess skills development.

Concept: Visual Discrimination

Activity: Match Cats
Duplicate sets of cards with pictures or designs on them are made with as many cards as there are players. The players sit on the surface area. The cards are passed out randomly. On a signal or music playing, the players move around the activity area with specified locomotor movements such as hopping or skipping. When the music stops or a signal is given, each player finds the person with his or her duplicate card, joins one hand, and they sit down together. The last couple down becomes the match Cats for that turn. The players then get up and exchange cards. The activity continues in the same manner with different locomotor movements used.

Application: Depending on the level of skills development of the children, the cards may be pictures of real objects or abstract forms, colors, alphabet letters, and words.

Concept: Visual Discrimination

Activity: Mother May I (Adaptation)
The players stand on a line at the back of the activity area. The teacher has cards showing object pairs, similar and different. The teacher holds up one pair of cards. If the paired objects or symbols are the same, the children may take one giant step forward. Any child who moves when he or she sees an unpaired set of cards must return to the starting line. The object of the activity is to reach the finish line of the opposite side of the playing area.

Application: The teacher may select cards to test any level of visual discrimination. Using pairs of cards for categorizing pictures would utilize concept and language development.

Concept: Visual Discrimination

Activity: Match Cards
Each player in the group is given a different-colored card. Several players are given duplicate cards. There are two chairs placed in the center of the activity area. On a signal, the players may walk, skip, hop, etc., to the music around the activity area. When the music stops the teacher holds up a card. Those children whose cards match the teacher's card run to sit in the chairs. Anyone who got a seat scores a point. The play resumes. Cards should be exchanged frequently among the players.

Application: This visual discrimination activity can be adapted easily to include increasing complexity of the visual discrimination task as well as how the children move about and the task for scoring points. Visual discrimination tasks might also include shapes, designs, and letters (both uppercase and lowercase).

Letter Recognition

Concept: Recognizing Letters of the Alphabet

Activity: Letter Spot
Pieces of paper with lowercase letters are placed in various spots around the activity area. There should be several pieces of paper with the same letters. The teacher has a number of large posters with the same, but capital letters. A poster is shown to the group. The players must identify the letter by name and then run to that letter on the floor. Any players who is left without a spot gets a point against him or her. Any player who has less than five points at the end of the specified time is considered a winner.

Application: Children are helped to associate letters with their names. After the activity the posters can be put on display around the activity area.

Concept: Recognizing Letters of the Alphabet

Activity: Call and Catch (variation)

The players stand in a circle. The leader stands in the center of the circle with a rubber ball. Each player is assigned a different letter. The letter may be written on a card attached to a string which the player wears as a necklace. Each player reads his or her letter before the activity is started. The leader calls out a letter and throws the ball into the air. The player who has that letter tries to catch the ball after it bounces. The leader can provide for individual differences of players. For the slower player the leader can call the letter and then momentarily hold the ball before throwing it into the air.

Application: This activity provides children the opportunity to become familiar with names and visual identification of letters. Later, the teacher could hold up letter cards rather than calling the letter. The children then might have to name the letter and catch the ball. Eventually, both upper- and lowercase cards might be used in the activity.

DIAGNOSING READING SKILLS THROUGH ACTIVE PLAY

As a child moves into the beginning reading skills, active play experiences continue to serve as a valuable means of assessing skill mastery. Skill areas as sight vocabulary, word-attack skills, alphabetical order, comprehension and vocabulary meaning can be developed through various dimensions of active play experiences. Likewise, level of skill mastery can also be assessed. Activities that utilize the various reading skills mentioned above are described in order to demonstrate the nature of active play experiences that can be employed.

Sight Vocabulary

Developing sight vocabulary through active play utilizes words and phrases from materials children are currently reading.

Concept: Sight Vocabulary

Activity: Call Phrase

The players form a circle, facing the center. They may be seated or standing. One player is designated as the caller and stands in the center of the circle. Each player is given a card with a phrase printed on it. Several players can have the same phrase. The caller draws a card from a box containing corresponding phrase cards and holds the card for everyone to see. When the phrase is read, this is the signal for the players in the circle with the same phrase to exchange places before the caller can fill in one of the vacant places in the circle. The remaining player becomes the caller.

Application: Children need opportunities to develop quick recognition of phrases. This activity provides the repetition necessary to help children develop familiarity with phrases they are meeting in their reading material. The phrases may be taken from group experience stories, readers, or children's own experience stories.

Word Attack

Word-attack skills assessed through active play experiences may include phonic elements of words, rhyming words, vowel letter patters, syllables, and endings.

Concept: Auditory Discrimination – Consonant Digraphs (ch, sh, th)

Activity: Mouse and Cheese

A round mousetrap is formed by the players standing in a circle. In the center of the mousetrap is placed the cheese (a ball or some other object). The players are then assigned one of the consonant digraphs sh, ch, or th. When the leader calls a word beginning with a consonant digraph, all the players with this digraph run around the circle and back to their original place, representing the holes in the trap. Through these original places they run into the circle to get the cheese. The player who gets the cheese is the winning mouse for that turn. Another word is called, and the same procedure is followed. Players may be reassigned digraphs from time to time.

Application: Children need repetition for developing the ability to hear and identify various sound elements within words. This activity enables children to recognize consonant digraphs within the context of whole words. A variation of this activity would be to have the teacher hold up word cards with words beginning with consonant digraphs rather than saying the word. This variation would provide emphasis on visual discrimination of initial consonant digraphs. Another variation would focus on ending consonant digraphs, either auditory or visual recognition.

Concept: Rhyming Words.

Activity: Rhyme Chase
    The players form a circle. Each player is given a card with a familiar word from the children's sight vocabulary written on it. The teacher may ask each player to pronounce his or her word before beginning the activity. The players should then listen and look at the words as each one identifies his or her word. The teacher then calls out a word that rhymes with one or several of the words held by the children. The child (or children) holds up the rhyming word so all the children can see it. This child must then give another word that rhymes with his or her word. This is a signal for all of the other children to run to a safety place previously designated. The child or children with the rhyming words try to tag any one of the children before he or she reaches a safe place. A child who is tagged receives a point. The object is to get the lowest score possible. Word cards can be exchanged among the children after several turns.
    Application: In this activity the children are called upon to relate auditory experiences in rhyming with visual presentations of these words. Sight vocabulary is also emphasized as the children reinforce the concept of visual patters in rhyming words.

Concept: Recognition of Visual Letter Patters – Vowel Sound Principles (Open, Closed, and Final e)

Activity: Letter Pattern Change
    The players are seated. Each player is given a card with a single-syllable word having one of the three vowel sound patterns (Examples: open-syllable pattern – a, he, go; closed-syllable pattern – get, bud, hip; final e pattern – game, lute, side). The teacher then holds up a word card with words also representing these patterns. Those children having words with the same letter patterns and the same vowel run to a chalkboard and write their word on the board and say it. Each child who is correct scores a point. Word cards should

be changed frequently among the children. Later, the teacher may have the children whose word has the same letter pattern come to the board without it having to have the same vowel.

Application: The activity provides the children the opportunity to practice recognition of visual letter patterns as cues to vowel sounds. Children can be called upon to identify the name of the vowel sound principle that their word represents, for example, open, closed, or final e. The vowel digraph letter pattern might also be included in this activity.

Alphabetical Order

Alphabetizing words is an essential skill for locating words in dictionaries or information in encyclopedias. Active play experiences utilizing the first two, three or four letters for alphabetizing can later be developed as the teacher assesses when there is skill mastery of the less difficult tasks of alphabetizing.

Concept: Alphabetical Order

Activity: Alphabet Lineup

The players are divided into teams. For each team a set of 26 cards, one for each letter of the alphabet, is placed out of order so as to be seen by all the players. The teams make rows at a specified distance from the letter display. A goal line is established at the back of the activity area for each team. The object of the activity is for each member, one at a time, to run and pick up a letter in correct alphabetical order, carry it to the team's goal line, and place the letter side by side in correct order. When each team member has found a letter, the team begins again until the alphabet is complete. The first team to complete placing the alphabet correctly at its goal line wins.

Application: Children need many different types of opportunities to practice putting the letters in correct alphabetical order. This activity provides a new way to practice this skill.

Comprehension

Vocabulary meaning as well as other comprehension skills such as in the following active play experience utilizing sequence of events can be emphasized in active play. "Sentence Relay" further serves as an example of how the buddy system can work in the active play approach.

Concept: Sequence of Events

Activity: Sentence Relay

Relay teams of five players each are selected to make rows before a starting line 10 to 15 feet from sentence charts for each team. The remaining players can serve as scorers. Each player on the team is given a sentence that fits into an overall sequence for the five sentences given a team. (The teams are given duplicate sentences.) Each sentence gives a clue to its position in the sentence sequence, either by idea content or word clue. On a given signal the team members get together and decide the correct sentence order. The player with the first sentence then runs to the sentence chart, places the sentence on the top line of the chart, underlines the key part of the sentence that gives the clue to the sequence, and returns to his or her team. The player with the next sentence then runs to place his or her sentence below the first sentence. This procedure continues until the sentences are in order. The team to complete the story with sentences in correct order first wins. The scorers check on the accuracy of the sentence order for each team. For the next game the scorers can exchange places with those who were on the teams. Variations of this activity can include the use of cartoons with each player being given one frame of the cartoon strip. To make the activity more difficult, more sentences may be added to the sequence. To prevent copying, the teacher can give different story sentences to each team.

Application: In this activity those children having difficulty with reading are helped by those who are more able readers and not eliminated from the activity. After the activity is played the teacher should go over the key elements in the sentences that provided clues to the proper sequence.

How might Sentence Relay be used for diagnosis? It might be used just as it is described above or certain adaptations might be made. In this case, the reading task in the active play experience is to recognize key elements in the sentences that provide clues to the proper sequence. The teacher can note whether a child is able to identify appropriate clues to sequence in his or her sentence. The teacher might observe which children perform the task easily and those who appear to need additional experiences in identifying key elements in sentences relating to sequence.

The activity might also be adapted by changing it to one that utilizes a story with several key sentences missing, the number of missing sentences being the same as the number of children on each team. The reading task would then be one of using context clues of a larger meaning unit to identify the proper order of sentences.

One of the many advantages of the active play approach is that it is fairly easy for the teacher to identify the specific reading skills being utilized in an activity which in turn facilitates assessment of children's mastery of that skill. In this way diagnostic teaching techniques aid a teacher's efforts to adjust the learning activities of the reading program to the needs of the children. The examples presented are representative of almost unlimited possibilities in structuring appropriate reading experiences for children. The creative teacher should be able to present text to the development level and skill needs of the children.

Chapter 9

Developing Reading Skills
through Active Play

The active play experiences in this chapter have been grouped by the major aspects of the reading program. Some of the activities are particularly useful for developing specific language or reading concepts. In these activities the learner acts out the concept and thus is able to visualize as well as get the *feel* of the concept. Other activities help to develop skills by using these skills in highly interesting and stimulating situations.

As in the previous chapter, the "Application" section for each activity indicates the appropriate use of this activity, whether for the development of a concept or for skill mastery.

Suggestions for adapting many of the activities are made in order to extend these types of activities to other elements of the various aspects of the reading program. The activities included have much versatility, depending on the creativeness of the adult using them

Word Analysis Skills

Concept: Recognizing Letters of the Alphabet

Activity: Letter Snatch

The players are divided into two teams of eight to ten each. The teams face each other about 10 to 12 feet apart. A small object such as a ball or beanbag is placed on the surface area between the two teams. The members of both teams are given letters. The leader then holds up a card with a letter on it. The players from each team who have the letter run out and try to grab the object and return to their line. If the player does so without being tagged by the other player, he or she scores two points. If tagged, the other team scores one point.

Application: Children have the opportunity to practice letter recognition in this activity. Visual matching can be with all small letters at first and then later with all capital letters. After the children have learned both small and capital letters, with the teacher displaying cards showing either type of letter.

Concept: Recognizing Letters of the Alphabet – Matching Capital and Small Letters

Activity: Large and Small

The players are divided into two teams of eight to ten each. The teams stand in lines about 15 feet apart and face in the same direction. The players on the first team are given a card with a small letter on it. Each member of the second team is given a card with the corresponding capital letters. The members of the first team hold their cards behind them for the second team to be able to see. The leader touches a player on the second team. This player then runs over to the first team, finds the player with the same letter as his or hers, and tags the player. The player on the first team turns and chases the child who tagged him or her who tries to get back into place before being touched by the other player. If tagged, the first team gets one point; if he or she gets back safely, team two gets one point. After each player on the second team has had an opportunity to match the letter, the leader gives the players on the first team the opportunity to match the letters. To do this, the teams should both face in the opposite direction so that the first team can now see the letters the players on the second team hold behind their backs.

Application: This activity provides the necessary experience in associating capital and small letters that children need to become more familiar with the letters of the alphabet in upper- and lowercase form.

Concept: Recognizing Letters of the Alphabet – Vowels

Activity: Magic Vowels

The playing area is considered the Magic Area. The vowels marked on it represent Magic Spots. The players make a single file and follow a leader around the area. When a stop signal is given, all of those on Magic Spots are safe and score a point if they can name the vowel on which they are standing. Those who are not standing on a Magic Spot or who cannot name the vowel do not score. The player with the most points wins.

Application: Children need opportunities to practice identification of the vowel letters. This activity provides the drill to aid in the recognition of the vowel letters. Children who are having difficulty are not eliminated from the activity and are thereby given the chance to continue practicing with the vowels until they become more familiar with them.

Concept: Auditory Discrimination – Beginning Sounds of Words

Activity: Match the Sound

A group of eight to ten players form a circle. They skip around in the circle until the leader gives a signal to stop. The leader then says a word and throws a ball directly at one of the players. The leader begins to count to ten. The player who catches the ball must say another word, which begins with the same sound before the leader counts to ten. If the player does, he or she gets a point. The player with the most points wins. The other players in the circle must listen carefully to be sure each player calls out a correct word. As the children learn to associate letter names with sounds, the child must not only call another word beginning with the same sound but also must identify the letter that the word begins with.

Application: This activity enable children to listen for sounds in the initial position of words. The activity can also be adapted to listening for final position sounds.

Concept: Auditory Discrimination – Consonant Blends

Activity: Crows and Cranes
The playing area is divided by a centerline. On opposite ends of the area are drawn base lines, parallel to the centerline. The group is divided into two teams. The players of one team are designated as Crows and take position on one side of the playing area, with the base line on their side of the centerline serving as their safety zone. The members of the other team are designated as Cranes and take position on the other side of the playing area, with their base line as a safety zone. The leader stands to one side of the playing area by the centerline. The leader then calls out "Cr-ranes" or "Cr-r-ows." In calling cranes or crows, the leader emphasizes the initial consonant blend. If the leader calls the Crows, they turn and run to their base line to avoid being tagged. The Cranes try to tag their opponents before they can cross their base line. The Cranes score a point for each Crow tagged. The Crows and Cranes then return to their places and the leader proceeds to call one of the groups: play continues in the same manner. This activity can be extended to include other words beginning with consonant blends, for example, swans and swallows, storks and starlings, squids and squabs.
Application: Repetition of the consonant blends during the activity helps children to become aware of these sounds and to develop their auditory perception of the blends of the context of words. Discovering names of animals with other consonant blends can help children in their ability to hear consonant blends in the initial position of words.

Concept: Auditory Discrimination – Consonant Blends

Activity: Call Blends
Eight to ten players stand in a circle. The leader stands in the center of the circle, holding a ball. Each player is assigned an initial consonant blend (st, bl, cl, and so forth). When the leader calls out a word with an initial consonant blend, the ball is thrown into the air. The player assigned that blend must then call a word using the blend and catch the ball after it has bounced once. Depending upon the ability level of the children, the leader can control the amount of time between calling out the blend word and the time the child catches the ball and calls out his or her word. When the child gives a correct word and catches the call, he or she scores a point. The child with the most

points wins. The leader can reassign blends frequently to the children during the activity.

Application: This activity is a supplemental one to reinforce previous auditory and visual presentation of consonant blends in the initial position. Blends used in the activity should be those with which the children have worked.

Concept: Auditory Discrimination – Final Consonant Blends (nk, ck, nd, st, nt, rst)

Activity: Final Blend Change

The players form a single circle, with one standing in the center of the circle. Those in the circle are designated as different final consonant blends. Several will be assigned the same blends. Each player may be given a card with his or her blend written on it to help remember. The leader then pronounces a word with one of the final position blends. All the players with this blend must hold up their card and then run to exchange places. The player in the center tries to get to one of the vacant places in the circle. The remaining player goes to the center.

Application: This activity helps children to develop their auditory discrimination of final position blends. They must listen carefully to the words pronounced. By holding up their card, they are associating the visual with the auditory symbol for that sound.

Concept: Auditory Discrimination – Vowels

Activity: Build a Word

The players are divided into several teams. The teams stand in rows behind a starting line 10 to 13 feet from a chalkboard. The leader calls a word. The first player on each team runs to the board and writes another word with that vowel sound on the board. He or she then returns to the team and tags the next player. The second player then writes a second word with the same vowel sound on the board. If an error is made, the leader helps the player correct it before the next player takes a turn. This procedure continues until every player has written a word on the board. The team finishing first scores a point. Another word is then called.

Application: This activity can be played when children have been introduced to vowel sounds, either a few or all of them. Words called by the leader reflect those vowels which the children have been practicing. Words can be called using only the short sounds of all the vowels, then the long sounds of all the vowels, then both long and short sounds of one vowel, and finally long and short sounds of all vowels. This activity can be adapted to practicing with initial and final consonants.

Concept: Rhyming Words

Activity: Rhyme Grab

The group is divided into two teams. The teams line up and face each other about 15 or 20 feet apart. A ball or beanbag is placed in the center of the area between the two teams. The members of each team are given corresponding rhyming words. The leader calls a word. The players who have words that rhyme with the one the leader calls try to snatch the ball. The player who gets the ball scores a point for his or her team. The team with the most points wins.

Application: Children need to have many situations that call upon their auditory skill in hearing words that rhyme. In this activity, children may also be given an opportunity to associate printed words with spoken words by having the leader alternate holding up word cards and the children determining if the word assigned them rhymes with the printed word, or giving the children word cards and the leader calling out words.

Concept: Initial Consonant Substitution

Activity: First Letter Change

The group is divided into several teams. The teams stand in rows behind a starting line 10 to 15 feet from a chalkboard. A word such as *ball* is written on the board for each team. (To prevent copying, different words should be used for each team.) On a signal the first player on each team goes to the board, says the word, writes another word, changing the initial consonant to make another meaningful word, says the word, and then runs to the rear of the team. The second player of the team repeats this same sequence. The first team to complete the writing of the words with initial consonant substitution correctly scores a point. Any child having trouble may ask the help of one member of his or her team to identify another word.

Application: Children are able to develop their skills in using initial consonant substitution in this activity with the added dimension of visual and kinesthetic experiences by seeing a word and writing new words, using different initial consonants.

Concept: Visual Discrimination – Whole Words

Activity: See the Same

The players are divided into two teams. Sets of word cards are made up and placed in a large, shallow box, one for each team. The words selected are those being developed as sight vocabulary. A pair of word cards is made up for each word. The words are then mixed up in the boxes. The two teams stand in rows behind a starting line. On a signal the first player of each team runs to the team's box and looks for two words that are alike. He or she then displays the pair of words on a sentence chart holder that is set up next to the team's box. The next player on the team proceeds in the same manner. The first team who has each player find a pair of words wins.

Application: Children need opportunities to visually match not only letters but also words in order for them to develop skills of seeing letter elements within the whole word. This activity provides an interesting means for developing this skill. The teacher may encourage the children to identify the word pair they have found. (If there are additional sentence chart holders, it is desirable to have smaller groups and thus more teams.)

Concept: Visual Discrimination – Whole Words

Activity: Cross the Bridge

The activity area is marked off with lines at each end. A player is selected to be the Bridge Keeper. He or she stands in the center of the area while the remainder of the group stands behind one end line. Each player is given a card with a sight vocabulary word on it. Several players should have the same word. The Bridge Keeper is given a box with a complete set of word cards that correspond to those given the other players and large enough for all players to see. The players call out to the Bridge Keeper; "May we use the

Bridge? May we use the Bridge?" The Bridge Keeper replies, "Yes, if you are this word." He or she then holds up one of the word cards from his or her box for all players to see. The player or players having that word try to cross to the other end line without being tagged by the Bridge Keeper. The procedure is continued again with other words. Those players tagged must help the Bridge Keeper to tag other players as they also try to cross the bridge. Occasionally, the Bridge Keeper may call out, "Everybody across the Bridge," when all the players may then run to the opposite end line. The activity can continue until one player remains. He or she becomes the Bridge Keeper for the next time, or another Bridge Keeper may be selected.

Application: This activity provides children the opportunity to match words visually as a means to reinforce words to the point that they may become a part of the child's sight vocabulary.

Concept: Auditory and Visual Association – Initial Consonants

Activity: Consonant Relay

The players are divided into several relay teams. The teams are a specific distance from a chalkboard and are seated. The leader stands so as to be seen by the players when pronouncing the words. The leader says a word beginning with a consonant sound. The last player on each team runs to the board, writes the beginning consonant, and returns to the head of his or her team. Each player moves back one place. The first player to get back to his or her seat with the correct letter written on the board scores a point for the team. The leader says another word, and the activity continues as above until everyone has had a turn. The team with the highest score wins.

Application: This activity gives children practice in hearing initial consonant sounds and associating them with their written symbols. The activity can be adapted to working with final consonants, digraphs, blends, and long and short vowel sounds.

Concept: Plurals of Nouns

Activity: Plural Relay

The group is divided into teams, which stand in rows 10 to 15 feet from a chalkboard. Each team has a different list of nouns placed on the board. On a signal the first player runs to the board and writes the plural of the first noun next to it. He or she returns to the rear of the team, and the second player runs to the board and writes the plural of the second noun, and so on. A player who is having difficulty may call upon one of the members of his or her team for help. The team that finishes first with all the plurals written correctly wins. At first, lists of nouns may just include regular plurals; later, words with irregular noun plurals may be added.

Application: This activity enable children to practice their skills in identifying plural forms of nouns. As irregular noun plurals are worked with, the children can be helped to note that not all nouns have the same plural endings. They can be helped to note that some nouns form their plurals by changing their spelling and that some nouns remain the same for the plural form.

Concept: Inflectional Endings – s, ed, ing

Activity: Ending Relay

The group is divided into teams. Each team is given a box filled with sight vocabulary words having *s, ed, ing* endings. The boxes are placed by a chalkboard. The teams make rows at a starting line 10 to 15 feet from the board. On a signal the first player of each team runs to the team's box and picks out three words; one with an *s* ending, one with *ed*, and one with an *ing* ending. He or she places the words along the chalk tray, pronounces each and returns to the team. The second player continues in the same manner. The team that finishes with the accurate selection and pronunciation of words first wins.

Application: This activity enables children to practice their skills in identifying visually presented words with different inflectional endings. The activity may later include words with irregular endings. It also provides reinforcement of sight vocabulary.

Concept: Dividing Words into Syllables

Activity: Syllable Relay

The players are divided into two teams. A captain is chosen for each team. The teams stand about 15 feet from a finish line. Each team is given a set of cards that have individual letters written on them. Each captain is given a red card. The leader holds up a card with a two-syllable word written on it large enough for all to see. If the two-syllable word contains five letters, the first five players on each team look for the correct letters in their set of cards, run to the finish line, and stand, holding their letters in correct order to spell the word. The captain then stands with his or her red card between the letters where the word is divided into syllables. The team making up the word with the proper designation for dividing it into syllables first scores a point. The next word is then given. The next group on the team finds the necessary letters and proceeds in the same manner. The team with the highest score wins.

Application: When children have had some experience with syllabication rules (vc/cv, v/cv, and v/cle), this activity can provide the necessary drill for reinforcing these rules. Those children having difficulty can be helped to see the vowel-consonant patterns in the words as they group themselves as letters and how the words are divided into syllables. In this activity the children having difficulty are helped by other members of the team rather than being eliminated.

Concept: Accent as Clues to Meaning

Activity: Accent Relay

The group is divided into several teams. The teams make rows behind a starting line 10 to 15 feet from a chalkboard. Complete sets of words (a few more than the number of players on the teams), divided into syllables and marked with accents, are written on the board. Examples of words to be used *ob'ject* and *object'*, *re'cord* and *record'*. The leader reads a sentence in which one of the words from the board is used. The first player on each team runs to the board and underlines the correct word as it was used in the leader's sentence. He or she then returns to the rear of the team. The first player to return scores a point for the team. The second player proceeds to underline a second word with the leader's reading of another sentence. This procedure continues until each player has had an opportunity to participate. The team with the most points wins. At any time a player is having difficulty, he or she may ask one member of the team for help.

Application: This activity helps children to listen carefully to words in the context of a sentence for clues to meaning. Children can also be helped to note the change of the function of these words in sentences when there is an accent change that of moving from a noun to a verb function.

SIGHT VOCABULARY

Concept: Sight Vocabulary

Activity: Word Carpet (Variation)
Several squares are drawn on the floor or pieces of paper are placed on the floor to represent Magic Carpets. Each Magic Carpet is numbered one to three to correspond with a numbered list of words on a chalkboard. The words include new vocabulary from the children's experience stories, readers, and social studies or science units. Two teams are selected, and each team forms a chain by holding hands. To music, the two teams walk around in circles and back and forth in a zigzag manner over the Magic Carpets until the music stops. Each player then standing on or closest to a Magic Carpet identifies any word from the numbered list on the board that corresponds with the number at that Magic Carpet. The leader then erases that word from the list, if it is read correctly. Each team scores one point for any correctly identified word. The team with the highest score wins.

Application: This activity provides an interesting experience whereby new words are given additional emphasis. To focus on meaning of new words, the teacher can require the child who has read a word correctly to put it in a sentence in order for the team to score an additional point. Children can also be helped to identify specific word analysis clues they used to identify their words.

Concept: Sight Vocabulary

Activity: Squirrel and Nut
All the players except one are seated with heads resting on an arm as though sleeping with one arm outstretched. The extra player is the Squirrel. The Squirrel who carries a nut (words on cards shaped like a nut) runs quietly about the room and drops a nut into the open hand of a player. The player jumps up from his or her seat, pronounces the word, and chases the Squirrel

who is safe only when he or she reaches his or her nest (seat). The activity continues with selection of a new Squirrel.

Application: Words selected for the activity may come from experience stories and stories read on that or the previous day. These kinds of activities provide the necessary repetition to develop instant recognition of words and can be used to maintain words in addition to word banks and word games that the children utilize.

COMPREHENSION

As important as sight vocabulary and word analysis skills are in reading, the bottom line, so to speak, is comprehension. Without it, reading is reduced to the "calling of words." Many people have difficulty defining comprehension as it applies to reading. I like to think of it as the process of correctly associating meaning with word symbols, or simply extracting meaning from the written or printed page. Comprehension also involves evaluation of this meaning, sorting out the correct meaning and organizing ideas as a selection is read. In addition, there should be retention of these ideas for possible use or reference in some future endeavor.

To accomplish comprehension as described here, it is important for children to develop certain comprehension skills. The following is a list of such *general* comprehension skills.

1. Getting Facts
2. Selecting Main Ideas
3. Organizing Main Ideas by Enumeration and Sequence
4. Following Directions
5. Drawing Inferences
6. Gaining Independence in Word Mastery
7. Building a Meaningful Vocabulary
8. Distinguishing Fact from Fantasy

In the following chapter, I will show how this list of comprehension skills can be used as an inventory for the adult to evaluate how well the child is practicing and maintaining comprehension skills in listening and/or reading.

Concept: Following Directions

Activity: Simon Days

The players stand about the play area facing the person who plays Simon. Every time Simon says to do something, the players must do it. However, if a command is given without the prefix "Simon says," the players must remain motionless. For example, when "Simon says take two steps," everyone must take two steps. But if Simon says, "Walk backward two steps," no one should move. If a player moves at the wrong time or turns in the wrong direction, the player puts one hand on his or her head. The second time he or she misses, the other hand is placed on the head. The third time he or she misses a point is scored against him or her. The more quickly the commands are given and the greater number of commands, the more difficult the activity will be. The player with the lowest score wins.

Application: This activity provides children the opportunity to follow oral directions in a highly motivating situation. The rules of the activity, as adapted, allow those children who need the practice, additional chances if they have points scored against them.

Concept: Following Directions

Activity: Do This, Do That

Flash cards of "Do This" and "Do That" are used in this activity. One player is selected to be the leader and stands in front of the group. The teacher holds up a flash card, and the leader makes a movement such as walking in place, running in place, swinging the arms, or hopping on one foot. The players follow the actions of the leader when the sign says, "Do This." When the teacher holds up the sign "Do That," the players must not move although the leader continues the action. A point is scored against a player who is caught moving. The leader can be changed frequently.

Application: This activity can be used to help children to read carefully in order to follow directions. Later, the activity can be adapted by having the leader display written directions on flash cards, for example, hop in place, jump once, walk in place, and the like.

Concept: Vocabulary Meaning – Colors

Activity: Rainbow

The players form a circle, facing the center. The players may be seated or standing. One player is designated the Caller and stands in the center of the circle. Instead of counting off by numbers, the players are given small pieces of paper of one of the basic colors. The Caller is given a set of word cards, one for each of the basic colors corresponding to the colors given the players in the circle. The Caller selects one word card and shows it. The players with this color attempt to change places while the Caller tries to get to one of the vacant places in the circle. The remaining player can become the new Caller or a Caller can be selected by the children. Those players with the two colors then run to change places, with the Caller again trying to get to one of the vacant places in the circle. At any time, the Caller may call out "Rainbow." When this call is given, everyone must change to a different position.

Application: Children need many opportunities to develop their recognition of words in activities of this nature in which they are associating the word with the concept the word represents. This activity can be simplified in order for it to become appropriate for a language development activity. The Caller can have just color cards matching those of the children. Later, when the children have learned to match colors, the Caller can call out the names of the colors.

Concept: Vocabulary Meaning – Over and Under

Activity: Over and Under Relay

The group is divided into several teams. They stand one behind the other, separated about one foot apart. A ball is given to the first player on each team, who stands at the head of the row. On a signal he or she passes the ball behind over the head and calls "over." The second player in the row takes the ball and passes it between the legs and calls "under." Number three in the row takes the ball and passes it over head and calls "over" and so on down the row until the last one receives the ball. He or she then runs to the head of the row and starts passing the ball back in the same manner. The team whose first person reaches the head of the row first wins.

Application: This activity helps children to dramatize the meaning of the words *over* and *under*. For a variation, the teacher can hold up a card with either *over* or *under* written on it to indicate how the ball should be passed by the child moving forward to the front of the team.

Concept: Vocabulary Meaning – Word Opposites

Activity: Word Change

The group is divided into two teams who line up at opposite ends of the playing area. Each player is given a word printed on a card. The words given to one team are the word opposites of the words given to the other team. One player is selected to be *It* and stands in the middle of the playing area. The leader calls out a word, and this word and its opposite run and try to exchange places. *It* attempts to get into one of the vacant places before the two players can exchange places. The remaining player can become *It* for the next time or a new *It* can be chosen.

Application: This activity focuses on the meaning of sight vocabulary words. It can be varied with emphasis on synonyms, with teams given words that are similar in meaning.

Concept: Vocabulary Meaning – Word Opposites

Activity: I'm Tall, I'm Small

The group forms a circle with one player in the center. This player stands with eyes closed. It may be helpful to have him or her blindfolded. The players in the circle walk around the circle singing or saying the following verse:

I'm tall; I'm very small,
I'm small; I'm very tall,
Sometimes I'm tall,
Sometimes I'm small,
Guess what I am now?

As the players walk and sing "tall," "very tall," or "small," or "very small," they stretch up or stoop down, depending on the words. At the end of the singing, the leader signals the players in the circle to assume a stretching or stooping position. The player in the center, still with eyes closed, guesses which position they have taken. For the next time another player is selected to be in the center.

Application: This movement song helps children to develop word meaning by acting out the words. Use of word opposites in this manner helps to dramatize the difference in the meaning of words. The words and actions can be changed to incorporate a larger number of "opposites," for example:

My hands are near; my hands are far,
Now they're far, now they're near,
Sometimes they're near,
Sometimes they're far.
Guess what they are now?

The examples presented are representative of almost unlimited possibilities in structuring reading learning experiences for children. The creative adult should be able to develop numerous activities by adapting those presented in this chapter to the developmental and skill needs of the children.

Chapter 10

ACTIVE PLAY READING CONTENT

The term *reading content* is easy to describe because it is simply concerned with the information that a given reading selection contains. Therefore, active play reading content provides for reading material that is oriented to active play situations. Stories of different lengths are prepared for various readability levels, and the content focuses upon any aspect of active play. Content can be concerned with such forms of active play as active games, rhythmic activities, and stunts.

One of the early, and possibly the first attempts to prepare active play reading content – at least as conceived here – is my work in this area. This work, begun several years ago, involved preparation of a number of active play stories. These stories were used with several hundred children, and on the basis of the findings of the studies, the following generalizations have been derived:

1. When a child is self-motivated and interested, he or she reads. In this case, the reading was done without the usual motivating devices such as picture clues and illustrations.
2. These active play stories were found to be extremely successful in stimulating interest in reading and at the same time improving the child's ability to read.
3. Because the material for these active play stories was scientifically selected and prepared, and tested, it is unique in the field of children's independent reading material. The outcomes have been most

satisfactory in terms of children's interest in reading content of this nature as well as motivation to read.

FROM LISTENING TO READING

Before getting directly into the use of active play reading content, I want to take into account the important relationship between listening and reading. An important thing to remember is that the comprehension skills for listening are the same as the comprehension skills for reading. The essential difference in these two receptive phases of language is in the form of *input* that is used. That is, listening is dependent upon the *auditory* (hearing) sense, and reading is dependent upon the *visual* (seeing) sense. Since the main goal of reading is comprehension, it is important to recognize that as children listen to active play situations and react to them, they are developing essential skills for reading.

This brings us to the important question, "Should parents and other adults read to children?" People who spend their time studying about this reply with an unqualified affirmative. That is, there seems to be solid evidence to support the idea that reading to children improves their vocabulary knowledge, reading comprehension, interest in reading, and the general quality of language development. I emphasize this at this point, because we shall see later that reading to children is an important dimension in the use of active play reading content.

THE APAV TECHNIQUE

My procedure for learning to read through the use of active play reading content is identified as the *APAV Technique*, several examples of which will be presented later. The APAV Technique involves a learning sequence of *auditory input* to *play* to *auditory-visual input*, as depicted in the following diagram.

Auditory → Play → Auditory-Visual

Essentially, this technique is a procedure for working through active play to develop comprehension first in listening and then in reading. The A → P aspect of APAV is a directed listening-thinking activity. The child first receives the thoughts and feelings in an active play story through the auditory sense by listening to the story read by an adult. Following this, the child engages in the active play experiences that are inherent in the story. By engaging in the active play experience, the development of comprehension becomes a part of the child's physical reality.

After the active play experience in the directed listening-thinking activity, the child moves to the final aspect of the APAV Technique (A-V), a combination of auditory and visual experience by listening to the story read by the adult and *reading along* with the adult. In this manner, comprehension is brought to the reading experience.

Although the sequence of listening to reading is a natural one, bridging the gap to the point of handling the verbal symbols required in reading poses various problems for many children. One of the outstanding features of the APAV Technique is that the active play experience helps to serve as a bridge between listening and reading by providing direct purposeful experience for the child through active play after listening to the story.

Following are several examples of stories that an adult can use in applying the APAV Technique. Remember, first you read the story to the child (or children), then with various degrees of adult guidance there is participation in the active play experience, and then the story is read together. This technique may be used with school age children who are encountering some difficulties with comprehension, and it can be used with immediate preschool children to help them gain some sight words and develop listening skills. As far as the latter is concerned, I have had very successful experiences with four to five year old children, finding that many of them can retain what they have listened to for a minimum of one week and sometimes even much longer.

ACTIVE GAME STORIES

Do What Jack Does

Can you do what Jack does?
In this game the children stand behind one another.
One child is Jack.
He is first.
Jack walks.

He jumps.
He hops.
He skips.
He runs.
The other children try to do everything Jack does.
It is fun to follow Jack.
He can go fast.
How can he do so many things?
Jack walks like a bear.
Sally misses.
Jack jumps like a rabbit.
John misses.
Jane is the last one to miss.
She is the Jack for the next game.
How long could you do what Jack does?

The Little Bees Have Fun

One day some bees got together.
They wanted to play a game.
They talked to each other.
One bee said, "Let each of us find a friend."
Each bee found a friend.
Each bee faced his friend.
One bee stood alone.
Her name was Busy Bee.
She was *It*.
Busy Bee said, "Buzz."
All bees found another friend.
Now he was Busy Bee.
They played and played.
Could you play this game like the bees?

Oswald Octopus and His Friends

Oswald Octopus lives in the sea.

He has a big head.
He has big eyes.
He has many long arms.
Oswald Octopus plays a game with the fish.
The fish go to one side.
Oswald Octopus says, "All fish swim."
The fish try to get to the other side.
Oswald Octopus says," All fish swim."
The fish try to get to the other side.
Oswald Octopus tries to catch them.
When a fish is caught, he helps Oswald.
They play until all fish are caught.
Then they play the game again.
Could you and other children play this game the way Oswald Octopus played with his fish friends?

Wilbur Woodchuck and His Cane

Wilbur Woodchuck hurt his leg.
He needed a cane.
At last his leg got better.
He did not need his cane.
He said, "I will find some friends. We will play a game with my cane."
Wilbur's friends stood in line.
Wilbur was in front of the line.
He stood the cane in front of him.
He held it with his hand.
He called a friend's name.
Wilbur let the cane fall.
His friend caught it before it hit the ground.
He took Wilbur's place.
They played for a long time.
Could you find something to use for a cane and play this game with other children?

Billy Bear in the Circle

Many bears played in the big woods.
The bears stood in a circle.
Billy Bear stood inside the circle.
Billy Bear was *It*.
The other bears held paws to make a circle.
Then Billy Bear tried to get out.
The other bears tried to keep Billy Bear in the circle.
At last Billy Bear got out.
He ran fast.
All the bears ran after Billy Bear.
That bear was *It* for the next game.
Now he was Billy Bear.
Could you play this game with other children?

Sally Squirrel

One day Sally Squirrel met some friends.
They wanted to run and play.
Sally's friends went to one end of the field.
Sally stayed in the center of the field.
She was *It*.
When Sally said, "Change," her friends ran to the other end.
Sally tried to tag them.
She tagged one.
Now he was Sally's helper.
Sally again said, "Change."
The squirrels ran back to the other end.
More squirrels were tagged.
They were Sally's helpers.
Each time Sally said, "Change," they ran to the other end.
They played until only one squirrel was left.
He was *It* for the next game.
Could you play this game with your friends?

The Chasing Game

Let's play a chasing game.
Children stand in a circle.
One child is in the center of the circle.
He closes his eyes.
He turns around and around.
He stops and points to a child.
This child runs.
All children chase him.
One child taps him.
He is *It* for the next game.
Could you play this game at school and at home?

The Kittens and the Ball of Yarn

Have you every heard of kittens playing with a ball of yarn?
They do many things with it.
Once some kittens found a ball of yarn.
This is what they did.
They stood close together in a circle.
The kittens in the circle passed the ball of yarn around.
Each kitten would take it.
He would try to pass it to the next kitten.
They tried to pass it quickly.
Do you know what the kitten outside the circle tried to do?
He ran around outside the circle.
He tried to tag the ball of yarn.
Once he did tag it.
Then he changed places with the kitten who had it.
They had fun with this game.
They played for a long time.
Could you use a rubber ball instead of a ball of yarn and play this game with other children?

Chippy Chipmunk and His Friends

One day Chippy Chipmunk met some of his chipmunk friends.

They stood around and talked.

After a time all except two of them stood together in a circle.

Chippy and Charlie Chipmunk went outside the circle.

Chippy Chipmunk began to chase Charlie.

Charlie stood in front of Chester Chipmunk.

Now Charlie chased Chester.

He tagged him before Chester stood in front of another chipmunk.

Chester then became the chaser.

Charlie became the runner.

This was because he had been tagged by Chester.

The chipmunks played until all had a chance to be a chaser and a runner.

Could you make a circle with some other children and play this game the way the chipmunks played it?

Jane's Dream

One night Jane had a dream.

She dreamed she saw some children playing a game.

Some of the children formed a circle.

Other children were in the center of the circle.

The children who formed the circle had a large rubber ball.

They tried to hit the children inside the circle with the ball.

They tried to hit below the waist.

They did this so the children inside the circle would not get hurt.

A child inside the circle was hit with the ball.

He changed places with the child who hit him.

They played and played.

Each time a child was hit he changed places with the child who hit him.

Jane awakened in the morning.

She remembered her dream.

If you were Jane how would you make the dream come true?

RHYTHMIC PLAY STORIES

Falling Leaves (Creative Rhythm)

Leaves fall.
They fall from the trees.
They fall to the ground.
Fall like leaves.
Down, down, down.
Down to the ground.
Quiet leaves.
Rest like leaves.
Could you dance like falling leaves?

The Growing Flowers (Creative Rhythm)

Flowers grow.
First they are seeds.
Be a seed.
Grow like a flower.
Grow and grow.
Keep growing.
Grow tall.
Now you are a flower.
Could you grow like a flower?

We Dance (Dance)

We hold hands.
We make a ring.
We swing our arms.
We swing.
We swing.
We take four steps in.
We take four steps out.
We drop hands.

We turn about.
Could you do this dance?

Clap and Tap (Dance)

I clap with my hands.
Clap, clap, clap.
I tap with my foot.
Tap, tap, tap.
I point my toe.
And around I go.
Clap, clap, clap.
Tap, tap, tap.
Could you do this dance with a friend?

Swing Around (Movement Song)

Do you know the song, "Mary Had a Little Lamb?"
There are other words to this tune.
Sing these words.
They will tell you what to do.
Take your partner's hand.
Sing all the words to the same tune as "Mary Had a Little Lamb."
Do what the words say.

Walk with partners round and round.
Walk around, walk around.
Swing your partner round and round.
Swing and swing around.
Skip with partner round and round.
Skip around, skip around.
Swing you partner round and round.
Swing and swing around.

Could you learn these words and then do the dance with a partner?

Swing your Partner (Movement Song)

Everyone knows "Farmer in the Dell."
Here is a new way to play it.
Find a partner.
Take your partner's hand.
Do what the words say.
Do it to the tun of "Farmer in the Dell."

We walk around and sing.
We walk around and sing.
We stop ourselves and turn about.
Then with our arms we swing.
We run around and sing.
We run around and sing.
We stop ourselves and turn about.
Then with our arms we swing.
We skip around and sing.
We skip around and sing.
We stop ourselves and turn about.
Then with our arms we swing.

Would you like to find a partner and do this dance?

We Make Up a Dance (Dance)

One day Miss Jones asked the children in her class if they would like to make up a dance.
The children were very happy because they liked to dance.
They thought they could start the dance by holding hands and making a circle.
After they made the circle, they all said.

Let us slide to the right.
Let us slide, slide, slide.
Let us slide to the left.
Let us slide, slide, slide.

Now let us turn to the right all the way around.
Now let us turn to the left and all sit down.

Could you get some other children to help work out this dance?

Swing and Swaying (Movement Song)

Can you swing and sway to music?
Here are new words to "Rock-A-Bye, Baby."
As you sing the words, can you think of different ways to swing and sway?

Swinging and swaying go to and fro.
Sway in the breeze, turn round as you go.
Swinging and swaying, go to and fro.

Could you do something different with you hands each time you swing and sway to this song?

Curly Cat Takes a Walk

Curly Cat is asleep.
Curly Cat opens his eyes.
Curly Cat takes a walk.
He walks with long steps.
He holds his head high.
He walks all around.
Try to walk like Curly Cat.
Put your hands on the floor.
Walk all around like Curly Cat.
Could you walk so you would look like Curly Cat?

Grizzly Bear

I saw a Grizzly Bear.
Grizzly Bear was at the zoo.

He walked and walked.
I can walk like Grizzly Bear.
I can put my hands on the floor.
I walk on my hands and feet.
I say, "Gr-Gr-Gr."
Could you walk so you would look like Grizzly Bear?

George Giraffe

There is a tall animal in a faraway land.
He has a long neck.
His name is George Giraffe.
You could look like him if you did this.
Place your arms high over your head.
Put your hands together.
Point to the front.
This will be his neck and head.
Now walk like a George Giraffe.
This is how.
Stand on your toes.
Walk with you legs straight.
Could you walk so you would look like George Giraffe?

The Jumping Rabbit

I can jump like a rabbit.
I sit like a rabbit.
I hold my hands on the floor.
Now I jump.
My feet come up to my hands.
I hold my hands on the floor.
I jump again.
I jump again and again.
How many rabbit jumps can you take?

The Spider

Have you ever watched the way a spider walks?
They have long legs.
They put them way out.
Try to walk like a spider.
Put your hands on the floor.
Keep you arms straight.
Walk to the front.
Walk to one side.
Walk to the other side.
Walk to the back.
Walk all around like a spider.
Would you like to try to walk like a spider?

Chester Crow

Chester Crow is a big black bird.
He can hop.
You can hop like Chester.
Bend you knees.
Put your arms out.
Your arms are wings.
Hop like Chester Crow.
How many crow hops can you take?

The Lame Puppy

I saw a lame puppy.
The lame puppy walked.
He held up one leg.
He walked on three legs.
I walk like a lame puppy.
I hold up one leg.
I walk around.
Could you walk like a lame puppy?

Susan Seal

Did you ever hear of a sea lion?
Sometimes it is called a seal.
It lives in the sea.
Sometimes it lives in the zoo.
There is one in the zoo called Susan Seal.
She likes to swim.
She can also walk on land.
Would you like to try to walk like Susan Seal?
Try it this way.
Put your hands on the floor.
Put your feet back.
Put your weight on your hands and on top of your toes.
Now walk on your hands and drag you legs.
This is the way to walk like Susan Seal.
Do you think you could walk like Susan Seal?

EVALUATING PRACTICE OF COMPREHENSION SKILLS

In the preceding chapter, I provided a list of general comprehension skills and indicated that I would show how this list could be used as an inventory to help the adult determine how well the child is practicing and maintaining comprehension skills for listening and/or reading.

Inventory of Listening and/or Reading Comprehension Skills

Directions: Check YES or NO to indicate proficiency or lack of proficiency with which the child is using skills.

SKILLS
Yes   No
_____   _____ 1. Getting Facts – Does the child understand what to do and how to do it?
_____   _____ 2. Selecting Main Idea – Does the child use succinct instructions in preparing for and doing the play activity?

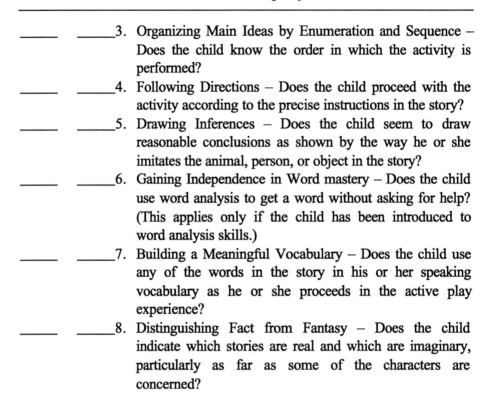

_____   _____3. Organizing Main Ideas by Enumeration and Sequence – Does the child know the order in which the activity is performed?

_____   _____4. Following Directions – Does the child proceed with the activity according to the precise instructions in the story?

_____   _____5. Drawing Inferences – Does the child seem to draw reasonable conclusions as shown by the way he or she imitates the animal, person, or object in the story?

_____   _____6. Gaining Independence in Word mastery – Does the child use word analysis to get a word without asking for help? (This applies only if the child has been introduced to word analysis skills.)

_____   _____7. Building a Meaningful Vocabulary – Does the child use any of the words in the story in his or her speaking vocabulary as he or she proceeds in the active play experience?

_____   _____8. Distinguishing Fact from Fantasy – Does the child indicate which stories are real and which are imaginary, particularly as far as some of the characters are concerned?

It should be recognized that different children will develop comprehension skills at different rates. Therefore, the adult should be patient and provide cheerful guidance as needed in assisting the child in performing the active play experiences depicted in the stories.

It is entirely possible that some adults will want to try to develop some of their own active play reading content, and I heartily recommend that you try your hand at it. Should this be the case, the following guidelines are submitted for consideration.

1. In general the *new* word load should be kept relatively low.
2. When new words are used, there should be as much repetition of these words as possible and appropriate.
3. Sentence length and lack of complex sentences should be considered in keeping the level of difficulty of material within the ability levels of children.

4. Consideration must be also given to the reading values and literary merits of a story. Using a character or characters in a story setting helps to develop interest.

5. The activity to be used in the story – particularly active game stories – should *not* be readily identifiable. When children identify an activity early in the story, there can be resulting minimum attention on their part to get the necessary details to engage in the active play experience. Thus, in developing an active play story, it is important that the nature of the activity and procedures for it unfold gradually.

I will conclude by stating again that all of the practices presented in this chapter have been carefully researched and extensively field-tested with large numbers of children. They have been found to meet with great success when applied in the appropriate manner.

Chapter 11

ALL ABOUT MATHEMATICS

The subject of mathematics in today's elementary schools, with the never-ending attempts at new methods and changes in content, is understandably bewildering to the conscientious teacher who must encounter every new and different procedure.

Over the years there have been many periods of change in mathematics in schools, and believe it or not, there was a time when mathematics was not even considered a proper subject of study for children. Since there has been so much confusion about the subject of mathematics I feel that it is appropriate to give an overview of "where we have been" and "where we think we are today" in mathematics.

In the very early days of this country, the ability to compute was regarded as appropriate for a person doing menial work, but such a skill was not viewed as appropriate for the aristocracy. Accordingly the study of mathematics was not emphasized in the early schools of America, not even the study of arithmetic.[1]

Gradually, as commerce increased, the ability to compute became increasingly valued and arithmetic became a part of the general education of the young, gaining an equal place in the curriculum with religion, reading, and writing. Late in the 18th century, laws to make arithmetic a mandatory school subject were passed in Massachusetts and New Hampshire. During this period, arithmetic was used primarily by businessmen and very gradually came into the schools of the day, and by 1800 arithmetic was taught quite generally in the schools. Arithmetic, as taught during the early decades of the new nation, consisted of working problems from rules. Only the teacher had a book, and the rules presented were applied largely to problems of commerce of that day. Arithmetic was seldom taught to children below 10 years of age, and, in fact, when a boy started to study the subject, it was considered a sign of approaching manhood.

The first two decades of the 19th century are sometimes considered as the lowest point in the history of American schools, particularly with the introduction of the Lancasterian system around 1812. In this system, teachers taught very large groups of children with the help of older children serving as monitors.

However, around 1820, the character of instructional practice began to change. This was largely due to the influence of Johann Heinrich Pestalozzi (1746-1827), the famous Swiss educator, whose ideas were enjoying great popularity in Europe and whose writings were beginning to appear in America.

Among the first texts to reflect the ideas of Pestalozzi were those authored by Warren Colburn. His text published in 1821, entitled *First Lessons in Arithmetic on the Plan of Pestalozzi*, gradually became the text par excellence for teaching arithmetic to children. Colburn attempted to use an approach that was more inductive. He sequenced topics better and instruction in arithmetic soon began at a much earlier age. Two major changes that Colburn introduced were (1) instruction sequenced from the concrete to the abstract, and (2) large numbers of drill exercises.

Another follower of Pestalozzi was A.W. Grube, a German whose texts became popular in parts of the United States in the mid-1800s. He and his followers advocated an inductive approach that made use of objects. They included all four arithmetical operations (addition, subtraction, multiplication, and division) in work with small numbers (1-10) before working with larger numbers.

As reformers, Colburn and Grube exerted less influence than might have been expected. Most of the arithmetic text writers and classroom teachers of the last half of the 19th century were influenced heavily by the faculty psychology of the phrenologists who believe the mind was composed of no less than 37 "faculties." These faculties included memory, reasoning, will, and the like. Each faculty was thought to be a kind of "mental muscle" for which continued exercise was needed if it was to develop. Joseph Ray's tests, which were very popular during this period, were based upon faculty psychology, as were the texts of Daniel Fish. In his suggestions for teachers in 1880, Fish stated, "The teaching of arithmetic must, therefore, to a great extent, be considered disciplinary, as training and developing certain faculties of the mind, and thus, enabling it to perform its function with accuracy and dispatch."[2]

It is not surprising that arithmetic was viewed by large numbers of children as something to be dreaded, for exercises were deliberately designed to be difficult in order to better "exercise" the mind. One page of Fish's 1871 text has addition examples, each with 25 five- and six-digit addends. Examples of written problems provided for children included the following: "What is the cost of 9-1/4 tons of coal, if .875 of a ton costs $5,635?" and "Bought 6/7 of a box of candles and having used 7/8 of them, sold the remainder for 16/25 of a dollar; how much would a box cost at the same rate?"[3]

It was thought that such problems would help children think clearly and quickly. It is questionable whether today's mathematics has yet completely recovered from the accompanying dread of arithmetic and the idea that "difficult is good" and "fun must be bad."

As schools became graded during the late 19th century, texts also became graded. Whereas a single text had been sufficient, texts were written for each grade level. The first such series appeared in 1877. They were written by Joseph Ray and were oriented toward faculty psychology. Graded texts resulted in more specific expectations at each level, locking teachers and children into material they were expected to cover. By the close of the 19th century, arithmetic instruction had become an "empty formalism."[4]

However, many individuals were seeking changes by the latter part of the century. The thinking of philosophers such as Herbart and James began to influence pedagogical thinking. The value of a formal discipline approach, based upon faculty psychology, was being questioned. Rather, attention was turning toward practical values. The Child Study Movement was also beginning to have its impact. It is not surprising that the period from 1890 to 1911 has been thought of as a period of reflection in mathematics education.

Several different movements have already left their mark on mathematics education during the 20th century, some running concurrently and others as a reaction to a different point of view. Teachers in today's schools, educated in different places and at different times, frequently continue to reflect the emphases of these various movements.

Early in the 20th century, problems in arithmetic books were of the type that were better suited to the social needs of the adult population and did not include the absurd problems found in texts in previous decades. On the other hand, students were expected to approximate 100 percent accuracy. Drill was no longer valued for "training the brain," but it was valued as a means of causing the child to think in terms of his or her own capabilities.

As time went on, there was more of an effort to restrict problems in arithmetic to those encountered in the normal daily lives of the adult population. It was felt that the school should think of arithmetic somewhat beyond the needs of adults. This procedure, known as the *social utility theory*, was greatly extended as research on the actual use of arithmetic began. Some of the advocates of social utility theory believed that with the program simplified, results should be much better and 100 percent mastery of the fundamentals should be expected.

The emphasis on social utility resulted in the development of problem units for different grades. For example, "a grocery store at school" in Grade 2; "the home garden, does it pay?" in Grade 4, and so on. Children studying arithmetic under the influence of social utility theory were not usually without drill exercises in the course of their progress through the grades, but arithmetic *was* understood to be something that would be used, and instruction often involved more informal child participation. (It is interesting to note that it was about this time – the late 1930s – that the use of games to teach arithmetic began to be encouraged. However, for the most part, these games were passive in nature and not necessarily those that I advocate, which I base on total or near-total physical response of the child.)

Before long, drill became to be emphasized less, for it was thought that mastery required less drill if learning occurred in a meaningful situation; thus, there came into being the *meaning theory*. This meant that there was a movement away from stressing only social meanings toward more of a stress on mathematical meanings. The term *meaning theory* is commonly associated with this movement, which had considerable impact on instruction in the 1940s and 1950s. It was reasoned that stress on socially useful arithmetic had too often been accompanied with rote instruction on the fundamentals and by drill, which made little mathematical sense to the child. Educators who promoted meaning theory stressed the need for helping children *understand* processes, and they taught that drill was to be used only to reinforce material the child already understood.

Over the years, the word *meaningful* has been used in so many different ways that confusion has understandably resulted. When the term is used to refer to instruction in which the mathematics makes sense to the child, that is, when he or she understands, *why*, then it is appropriate to contrast meaningful instruction with rote instruction. However, since the 1930s, meaningful instruction has often been contrasted with drill or practice. As a result, dangerously little practice has been included in some programs.

Changes in elementary school mathematics programs since the mid-1950s have been rather dramatic. These changes can be viewed as an acceleration of the changes toward more mathematically meaningful instruction that had taken place during the previous two decades, perhaps with a change in focus. Several factors converged to help bring about the "revolution" that occurred.

First of all, mathematics itself had changed, and attempts to unify mathematical concepts led to new basic structures that had not yet been reflected in mathematics instruction below the university level. Another contributing factor was the accumulating information about how children learn. For it was becoming well-established that children *could* learn quite complex concepts, often at a younger age. Other factors cited include the concern that the mathematics curriculum was largely the result of historical development rather than logical development, the increasing need for an understanding of mathematics by people in business and industry, and a belief on the part of many people that there was an overemphasis on computational skills.

The elementary school mathematics programs that developed during the late 1950s and the 1960s focused heavily upon concepts and principles and became immediately known as the *new math*. The content of programs for elementary school children contained more algebraic ideas and more geometry than had been included in previous years. In addition, such things as relationship between operations were stressed.

When the *new math* was introduced into the American education system it was probably one of the greatest upheavals in curriculum content and procedures in modern times. It also became the victim of much ridicule by educators and laymen alike. One night club entertainer was prompted to describe the purpose of *new math* as "to get the idea, *rather* than the right answer." One of my own mathematical friends, on comparing the *old math* and the *new math*, inferred that in the *old math* "they knew how to do it but didn't know what they were doing;" whereas in the *new math*, they know what they are doing, but they don't know how to do it."

In general, the *new math* was intended to do away with a process that had focused upon rote memory and meaningless computation. Further, it was expected that the new process would make it easier for students to develop mathematical understandings. The extent to which the *new math* achieved success has been challenged by some. Obviously, most educational innovations rightly have been criticized when one gives consideration to the extremes that are possible in any educational process. Because of this, it now appears that attempts are being made to reach some sort of happy medium. While it is not likely that anyone wishes to revert entirely to the *old math ways*, at the same time, it would be desirable to avoid some of the extremes that have brought harsh criticisms of the *new math ways*.

In modern times, a number of different mathematics programs have emerged. Among them are *Connected Mathematics Program* and *Core-Plus Mathematics Project*. The Connected Mathematics Program currently has been receiving a great deal of attention. However, it is not without its critics. One such criticism is that it entirely omits the important topic of *division of fractions*.

It appears that present approaches to mathematics programs for children are such that attempts are being directed toward situations that are more suited to the everyday facts of life. It is the premise of the present author that the active play approach to learning about mathematics not only deals with the everyday facts of life, *but with life itself* – at least as far as the child is concerned.

MATHEMATICS READINESS

We hear a great deal about *reading readiness*, but not nearly enough about *mathematics readiness*. There are certain *developmental tasks* that are important for children to accomplish. Mathematics can be considered as such a developmental task. That is, it is a task that a child needs to perform to satisfy his or her personal needs as well as those requirements that society and the culture impose upon the child. In viewing mathematics as a developmental task, we then can consider mathematics readiness as a developmental *stage* at which certain factors have prepared the child for mathematics. For example, a child probably is not ready to take on the task of addition if he or she has to count objects to get a sum. Likewise, if the child must add to find the product of two numbers, he or she is not yet ready for multiplication. Therefore, it seems that for the child to achieve mathematics readiness, time should be allowed for maturation of mental abilities and stimulation through experience. It might be said that *experience* is the key to the degree of mathematics readiness a child has attained upon entering school. In fact, research consistently shows that experience is a very important factor in readiness for learning in mathematics. It should be obvious that most of this experience will be the result of efforts of parents and others (siblings and other relatives) in the out-of-school situation.

Because of experiences in mathematics – or lack thereof – children entering the first grade vary a great deal in the amount of mathematical learning they bring with them. It is becoming a more or less common practice in many schools for teachers to try to determine how *ready* children are to deal with mathematics as they begin the first grade. This gives the teacher an idea of the needs of the children with regard to instruction.

To give the reader some idea of how a teacher might proceed, several *diagnostic* items in the area of mathematics are given here. (It should be clearly understood that these are not standard procedures, but merely representative examples of what teachers might do to help them determine how well-acquainted the children are with some of the mathematical experiences that will be dealt with as they begin their formal education.)

Ordinarily, these items are administered orally with small groups of children. The teacher tries to observe certain behavioral responses of children, such as hesitation in answering, inattention, lack of ability in following directions, or anything that could be interpreted as immature thinking.

Generally speaking, teachers are concerned specifically with such features as counting, number symbols, number order, ordinal use of numbers, understanding the simple fraction of ½, recognition of coins, and quantitative thinking.

The teacher might try to diagnose ability in *counting* by having children respond to such questions as the following: Can anyone count to find out how many boys are in our class? Can anyone count to find out how many windows there are in our room? Can anyone tell us how many chairs we have? Can anyone tell how many pictures we have in our room? The teacher observes those children who volunteer and the correctness of their responses. Different children are given an opportunity to answer the questions, and each time the responses are observed by the teacher.

In the area of *number symbols*, a teacher might use a procedure like the following: Ten cards with each card having a number (1-10) are placed on the chalkboard tray. The teacher then asks questions such as: Who can find the card that tells us how many ears we have? What is the number? Who can find the card that tells us how many arms we have? What is the number? Which card tells us how many fingers we have on one hand? What is the number? Which card tells us how many doors there are in the room? What is the number?

In checking the children for their knowledge of *number order*, the same procedure is followed except that the card numbers are out of order. Such questions as the following may be asked: Can you help me put these cards back in order? Another procedure used is to ask questions such as: What is the number that comes right after three? After six? After four? What is the number that comes right before seven? Before 10? Before five? What is the number that comes between one and three? Between six and eight?

Ordinal numbers are used to show order or succession such as first, second, and so on. This can be diagnosed by placing number cards from 1 to 6 in order along the chalkboard tray. The teacher then may ask: Who can tell me the *first* card? The *fifth* card? The *third* card?

To help determine how well the children understand the concept of one half, the teacher can use six equal sized glasses. One glass can be full, one can be empty, and the rest of the glasses can be one-fourth full, one-third full, one-half full, and three-fourths full. Such questions as the following can be asked? Who can tell me which glass is full? Who can tell me which glass is empty? Who can tell me which glass is half full? Who can tell me which glass is less than half full? Can you find a glass that is more than one-half full?

In diagnosing children's knowledge about *coins* the teacher can have 10 pennies, one nickel, and one dime. The teacher holds up each one of coins to see if the children can identify them. Such questions as the following can be asked: Does a penny buy less than a nickel? Does a dime buy more than a nickel? Which buys more, a penny or a dime? Would you give a nickel for four pennies? Would you give a dime for eight pennies?

The reason for presenting the above information is to give the reader an opportunity to just what might possibly be expected of a child in terms of mathematical understanding upon entering school.

NOTES

[1] No doubt the reason for this was that about this time elementary schools were beginning to include more advanced forms of mathematical processes in addition to the traditional study of arithmetic, which is considered to be a branch of the broader areas of mathematics.

[2] Fish, Daniel W., *The Complete Arithmetic*, New York, Ivison, Blakeman, Taylor & Co., 1880, p. vi.

[3] Fish, Daniel W., *Robinson's Progressive Practical Arithmetic*, New York, Ivison, Blakeman, Taylor & Co., 1871, pp. 115, 180.

[4] DeVault, M. Vere and Driewall, Thomas E., *Perspectives in Elementary School Mathematics*, Columbus, Ohio, Charles E. Merrill Publishing Company, 1969, p. 10.

Chapter 12

DEVELOPING CONCEPTS OF NUMERATION SYSTEMS THROUGH ACTIVE PLAY

Opportunities for counting and using numbers abound in many children's active play experiences. For example, in tag games the children who are caught can be counted and that number compared to the number of children not caught. In activities requiring scoring there are opportunities for counting and recording numbers. In fact, it is difficult to identify any kind of active play experience that does not include the use of numbers.

In this chapter many active play experiences are described. For each activity the mathematical concepts involved are noted so that adults can more easily locate instructional activities for a given content area. Furthermore, suggested applications for making the best use of each activity are included. Some of the activities are especially useful for introducing a mathematical concept. These involve the learner actively and incorporate a dramatization of the concept physically. Others reinforce concepts and skills previously taught. These are activities that provide needed practice in interesting and personally involving situations. Of course, adults will want to adapt many of the activities so they can be used to develop mathematical concepts and skills other than those cited in the descriptions.

The activities described in this chapter involve basic number and numeration concepts. In Chapter 13, activities are described that involve the operations of arithmetic: addition, subtraction, multiplication, and division. In Chapter 14 activities are presented that involved other areas of mathematics, included geometry and measurement.

CONCEPTS: ROTE COUNTING, FORWARD AND BACKWARD; ORDINAL NUMBER IDEAS; NUMERATION

Activity: Pass Ball Relay

Children divide into teams. The team members form rows close enough so they can easily pass a ball overhead to the next child in the row. On signal, a ball is passed over each child's head to the end of the row. As children pass the ball overhead, each child calls out the number of his or her position on the team (one, two, three, etc.) until the ball reaches the end of the row. When the last child on the team receives the ball, he or she calls his or her number, and then the ball continues to be passed forward to the front of the team. The activity can be varied by passing the ball in different ways: for example, under the legs, or alternating over and under. The winner is the first team to pass the ball forward and backward with correct counting both forward and backwards.

Application: Children gain skill in rote counting while engaged in this activity. Children *do* need to know the sequence of number names if they are going to be able to use that sequence for rational counting and in their study of arithmetic. The adult may start the counting at any number, depending on the skills of the group. Teams of 10 to 15 children can apply numeration concepts when the counting starts with numbers like 195 or 995.

CONCEPTS: ROTE COUNTING; COUNTING BY TENS; CARDINAL AND ORDINAL NUMBER IDEA

Activity: Bouncing Relay

The children are divided into several teams. Members of each team stand side by side. The first child bounces a rubber ball ten times consecutively, calling out the number of each bounce. When ten has been counted the ball is passed to the second child. The second child then bounces the ball ten times, calling out each bounce, but on the tenth bounce calls out "twenty," for that is the total number of bounces for the team. All team members follow the same pattern (1, 2, 3...9, 30) until each person has bounced the ball and added ten to each correct total. For example, if there are eight children on a team, the last child should end the count with "eighty." At any time a child misses before completing ten bounces, he or she retrieves the ball and continues counting. The first team reaching the correct total wins.

Application: Children gain needed skill in counting both ones and tens. Further, counting with each bounce helps to develop cardinal number concepts, for as a child says "five" he or she is completing five bounces, and as multiples of ten are called the child is stating the total number of bounces for the team.

CONCEPTS: RATIONAL COUNTING (0-9); NUMERALS (0-9)

Activity: Hot Spot

Pieces of paper (cardboard, asphalt tile) with numerals from zero through nine are placed in various spots around the activity area. There should be several pieces of paper for each numeral. The adult has a number of large posters with collections of objects pictured on them, including posters with no objects pictured. (An overhead projector may be used to present the different quantities of objects.) A poster is shown to the group, perhaps with the question, "How many?" The children must identify the number of objects on the poster and then run to that numeral on the surface area. Any child who is left without a spot gets a point scored against him or her. Any child who has less than five points at the end of the period of play is considered the winner.

Application: Children gain skill in counting a set of objects and identifying the digit that show how many are in a set. After the activity the posters can be put on display with the correct numeral by each one.

CONCEPT: QUANTITATIVE ASPECTS OF NUMBERS AND NUMERAL RECOGNITION

Activity: I Want to Meet

Ten cards are prepared so that each of the numerals one through ten will appear on one card only. Distribute these cards, one to each player. Then give each of the other players a number of objects (pegs, cards, paper clips), making sure that each of the quantities one through ten is represented at least once. The adult calls out a number, as four, and asks a player who holds the card having the numeral on it to go to the front of the group and hold his or her card for all to see. The player then says, "I want to meet all fours." The players with four objects hold them up. Someone counts them, and those who hold the correct number of objects join the player who is holding the card with the numeral 4 on it. They then run to a goal at the opposite end of the activity area. The first player to reach the goal scores a point. The activity continues with other numbers called. From time to time the adult should change the objects and cards held by the players. The first player to score a specified number of points wins.

Application: This activity provides a personally involving and interesting situation to relate numerals with the quantitative aspect of numbers. Children can be helped to count out the number of objects they have.

CONCEPTS: RATIONAL COUNTING (1-6); NUMERALS (1-6)

Activity: Watch the Numerals

On large sheets of paper write the numerals 1, 2, 3, 4, 5, and 6, one numeral per sheet. Be sure to make the numerals large enough that players can read them while walking around the activity area. Players start the activity by walking around to music in single file. Then the adult holds up one of the numerals. If the numeral is two, each player tries to find a partner, and they continue walking in pairs. If the numeral is three, the players walk in three's. If a player is not able to become a part of a grouping he or she goes to the sideline until the next numeral is presented, then he or she joins the scramble to get into a correct grouping.

Application: Children can gain skill in recognizing the numerals 1-6 and in forming groups for the number indicated. Be alert for the child who is challenged by having to be included within the group he or she is forming.

CONCEPTS: RATIONAL COUNTING; GREATER THAN; LESS THAN

Activity: Bee Sting

Three players are bees. They are in their hives marked on the activity area. The rest of the players are in the center of the area. The bees run out and try to catch (sting) the players. When a player is caught, he or she must go with the bee to the bee's hive. When all the players are caught, each bee counts those in his or her hive. Different players should have a chance to be bees.

Application: Children are provided an opportunity to practice rational counting. The relations greater than and less than are applied as the numbers of children in the hives are compared.

CONCEPTS: RATIONAL COUNTING; IDENTIFYING NUMERALS AND NUMBER WORDS FOR A GIVEN SET (0-9); READING NUMERALS AND NUMBER WORDS (0-9); ZERO AS THE NUMBER OF THE EMPTY SET

Activity: Show Me Relay

Teams of three players each participate in this relay. The teams make rows behind a starting line, and a chair is placed at a distance for each team. The first team member has a bag of objects such as beans, plastic discs, small cubes; the second has ten numeral cards, one each for the numbers zero through nine. If he or she calls out, "Show me five," the first player races to the chair, places five objects on the chair, and returns to touch the hand of the second player. The second player places the numeral for five on the chair, places five objects on the chair, and the third player places the number word card for five on the chair. A team is finished when the third player returns to the starting line. Whenever the leader calls "Show me zero," the first player touches the chair but, of course, does not leave any objects on it. The first team to finish and have the correct materials on the chair gets one point. A team that finishes first but does not have the correct materials on the chair loses a point. The first team to get five points wins the game. Roles of the team members should be exchanged from time to time.

Application: Children gain skill in matching sets with the numerals and number words which show how many are in a set. If children are permitted to assist the leader in verifying that the winning team has placed the correct material on their chair, practice is also provided in rational counting and oral reading of both numeral and number words for zero through nine.

CONCEPTS: RATIONAL COUNTING; PAIRS OF ADDENDS TO TEN; MISSING ADDENDS; COLUMN ADDITION

Activity: Count the Pins

Plastic bowling pins or similar objects are set up at one end of the activity area. These pins are arranged with four in the back row, three in the next row, two in the next, and one in the front. When they set up they form a triangle. Each player has a specified number of turns to roll a plastic ball. He or she stands behind a line a given distance away to roll. The total number of pins knocked down is his or her score. A total score is determined for each player.

Application: Children gain skill in rational counting as they count the number of pins knocked down. For variety, have the children count the number of pins that remain standing and apply their knowledge of addend pairs for ten in determining how many were knocked down. For example, if four remain standing, say "There are ten pins altogether. If one part of ten is four, what is the other part: Yes four and six is ten." If possible, children should be encouraged to add their scores to obtain their total score, thereby gain experience with column addition.

CONCEPTS: RATIONAL COUNTING; READING NUMERALS

Activity: Count and Go

The players line up along the long side of rectangular hard surface activity area. There are parallel lines drawn in chalk on the activity area. These are unequal distances apart, and parallel to the long side of the activity area. The leader stands across from the players with numeral cards. As the leader holds up any card at random (numerals on the cards are from one to the number of chalk lines which are drawn), the players must count the lines as they run toward the leader. When the players have progressed as many lines as indicated by the numeral card, they stop and stand still. The player who reaches the far side first is the winner.

Application: Reading numerals and rational counting is reinforced as children move forward the varying number of lines indicated on the card. The activity can be varied by relating the direction to move to the operation of addition and subtraction, as is often done with a number line. Directions, such as *plus two* and *minus three*, could be presented, and the children would then proceed to carry out these directions in terms of moving forward or backward.

CONCEPT: QUANTITATIVE ASPECTS
OF NUMBERS AND COUNTING

Activity: Come with Me

The players stand close together in a circle. One player is *It*. It goes around the outside of the circle. *It* touches a player and says, "Come with me." That player follows *It*. It continues in the same manner, tapping players who then follow *It* as he or she goes around the outside of the circle. At any time *It* may call, "Go home!" All the players following *It*, and also *It* runs to find a vacant place in the circle. The remaining player becomes *It* for the next time. At the beginning the leader has the player count how many there are at the start. *It* can count the players as he or she taps them. All the players also can be encouraged to count as *It* tags players. The number of players not tagged might also be counted.

Application: The children are able to practice counting varying size groups in this activity. By having *It* and all the children count as the children are tagged, each child is helped to see number names related to specific objects (in this case the objects are children).

CONCEPTS: GREATER THAN; LESS THAN; ORDINAL NUMBER IDEAS; EVEN AND ODD NUMBERS

Activity: Number Man

One child, the Number Man, faces the group which is standing on a line at the end of the activity area. Each player in the line is given a number by counting off – 1, 2, 3, 4, etc. The Number Man calls, "All numbers greater than _____" The players who have numbers greater than the one called must try to get to the other side of the activity area without being tagged by the Number Man. The Number Man may also call, "All numbers less than _____." "All odd numbers." "All even numbers." Anyone who is tagged must help the Number Man tag the runners. Any player who runs out of turn is considered tagged.

Application: Children gain skill with number sequence while identifying numbers which are greater or less than a given number. When children are lined up in sequence, it can be observed that the sets of odd and even numbers involved every other whole number.

CONCEPT: COUNTING – IN MULTIPLES OF ONE'S, TWO'S, FIVE'S

Activity: Count, Move, and Stop

One player is *It*. He or she stands behind a finish line. All the other players are at a starting lines that is drawn 25 to 50 feet away, parallel to the finish line. The players sit in a cross-legged position, arms crossed on chests, at the starting line. The player who is *It* hides the eyes and counts to ten (20 or 100, depending upon the skills of the group) in any way he or she chooses, by one's, two's, or five's. While *It* is counting, the players come to a standing position and move forward toward the finish line during the count. *It* must call the numbers loudly enough for all to hear. At the call of ten (or whatever number has been decided upon), *It* opens the eyes. All players must be seated cross-legged and with arms crossed on the chest, at the point to which they have advance. Any player caught out of position must return to the starting line and begin again. The activity continues in this manner until one player has crossed the finish line and is seated before *It* has completed the count. The first player over the finish line interrupts the count by calling "over." All players return to the starting line, and activity begins over again with this player as the new *It*.

Application: The activity provides the necessary repetition of counting by one's, two's, and five's for each child, since not only is *It* counting but each child is counting in order to determine his or her movement forward.

CONCEPTS: ORDINAL NUMBER IDEAS; MULTIPLES OF THREE

Activity: Leader Ball

Two teams stand in circle formation. On a given signal the leader of each team passes a ball to the player of his or her right, who passes it to the next player, and so on until it reaches the leader. The leader calls, "first round" immediately and continues to pass the ball for the "second round" and "third round." At the end of the third round, the leader raises ball to signify that his or her team has finished. A point is scored for the team finishing first.

Application: The time interval between "first round," "second round," and "third round" requires that children keep in mind which number comes next. A variation requires that after three rounds of play the ball is raised and a point is awarded, as above; however, the numbering of the rounds continues successively. During the second period of play, the leader counts fourth round, fifth round, and sixth round. Attention is drawn to numbers that are multiples of three.

CONCEPT: ORDINAL NUMBERS

Activity: Fetch and Carry

Two lines are drawn about 25 feet apart, one a starting line and the other goal line. The group is divided into teams of six. With a large group there will be several teams. Each member of the team is assigned a position, for example, first, second, through sixth. It might be helpful for some players to have each player as he or she stands in line, to call off the ordinal number of his or her position. In doing this they can be helped to understand what ordinal numbers mean. The object of the activity is for each team to get all its members from the starting line to the goal line. The teams line up at the starting line, facing the goal line. One a signal the first player on each team calls out his or her ordinal number and takes the hand of the second player and runs with him or her to the goal line. The first player remains there. The second player runs back to the team, calls out his or her ordinal number, taking the hand of the third player on the team. They run to the goal line. Now the second player remains there while the third player returns to get the fourth team member. This procedure continues until one team wins by getting all of its member across the goal line and in correct order first.

Application: This acting out of ordinal numbers makes it easier to understand the concept of position and sequence of numbers.

Chapter 13

DEVELOPING CONCEPTS OF ARITHMETICAL
OPERATIONS THROUGH ACTIVE PLAY

Active play activities can provide children with valuable experiences with the operations of arithmetic (addition, subtraction, multiplication, and division). The energetic involvement of children in such activities brings an interest and enthusiasm to the learning of arithmetic that many children need very much.

In this chapter, activities are described which incorporate the operations of arithmetic. Some activities involve the child with the meaning of the operation, and other activities include computing. For example, addition and subtraction are used in many activities that require scoring. For a given operation, activities focusing on the meaning of the operation should be incorporated into the instructional program before activities including computation.

In order to make it easier to find instructional activities for a given operation, the mathematical concepts involved in each are listed with the description of the activity. Also each description is followed by a discussion designed to help adult leaders make the best possible application of the instructional activity. These leaders will want to be alert to opportunities to further extend the mathematical experiences of children with these activities by keeping records, charts, and graphs, and by developing concepts of average and percentage.

Some of the activities are useful for introducing a concept. They involve the child actively and tend to incorporate a dramatization of the concept physically. Many of the activities provide reinforcement for concepts and skills, which have been introduced earlier. Children find such practice interesting, and they become eager participants in such learning experiences.

Adult leaders should feel free to adapt an activity, making it more appropriate for the developmental level of children. Often, by merely substituting a larger or smaller number, an activity can be made useful for a specific group of children.

CONCEPT: ADDITION

Activity: Three Deep

The players stand by two's one behind the other, in a circle. All face the center. A runner and a chaser stand outside the circle. The chaser tries to tag the runner. In order to be saved, the runner may run around the circle and stand in front of one of the couples in the circle. This makes the group three deep, and the player of the couple must now run. He or she is then chased and tries to save him or herself in the same way. The outside person in a group of three must always run. If the runner is tagged, he or she becomes the chaser and must turn and chase the new runner.

Application: The adult assists the children in identifying groups of two's when the circle is formed for the activity. When a runner stands in front of the group, the adult assists the children to identify that two and one make three.

CONCEPTS: MEANING OF ADDITION; NUMBER SENTENCES; EQUALS

Activity: Lions and Hunters

Two teams are established. One team, the hunters, begins by forming a large circle. The other team, the lions, is within the circle. The hunters use a large ball such as a beach ball and attempt to hit as many lions as possible within a two-minute period. As the lions are hit, they go to the lion cage that has been marked in chalk on the activity area. When the teams change places, the second group of lions hit go to a second lion cage marked on the activity area. A scorer records the number of lions by each cage and completes the appropriate number sentence and labels as illustrated:

(cage)		(cage)		
3	+	4	=	7
addend	plus	addend	equals	sum

Note: In an activity of this nature children should be cautioned to hit below the waist with the ball.

Application: Involve all of the children in counting the lions in each cage and in counting the number of lions caught altogether. Emphasize the fact that "three plus four" tells how many lions were caught altogether, and both names for the same number, and that is what "equals" means: it means "is the same as." Three plus four *is the same as seven*.

CONCEPTS: ADDITION; SUBTRACTION

Activity: Add-A-Number Relay

The group is divided into several teams, and a number is recorded to each team on a chalkboard. (Use low, one-digit numbers at first.) The adult writes or calls out a number, then the first team member of each team runs to the board and adds this number to his or her team's number on the board. He or she returns to the team, and the next team member runs to the board and adds a number to the new sum. Each player on the team does the same until the first team finished wins. Each team should start with different numbers to prevent copying. Size of numbers used will depend on the developmental level of the players.

Application: This activity provides reinforcement of addition facts and addition computation presented visually. Wide variation in the difficulty of the addition situation is possible by varying the numbers used. The same activity can be varied by using subtraction. When subtraction is the operation, be sure that the numbers recorded initially on the chalkboard are large enough to allow successive subtractions as indicated. The subtraction game is called "Subtract-A-Number Relay."

CONCEPTS: BASIC NUMBER FACTS;
BASIC SUBTRACTION FACTS

Activity: Number Catch

Every player is given a number from one to ten. The adult calls "Two plus two" or "Six plus one" and tosses a ball into the air. Any player whose number happens to be the sum of the numbers called can catch the ball. The other players run away as fast as they can until the player catches the ball may take three long, running strides in any direction toward the players. He or she then throws the ball, trying to hit one of the players (below the waist). If successful, the player who is hit has one point scored against him or her. The activity continues, with the adult calling out another pair of addends. The players with the lowest number of points are the winners.

Application: This reinforcement activity encourages immediate recall rather than just figuring out the sum again. Assign the numbers nine through eighteen if the children have studied the basic addition facts with larger sums. If the activity is altered for the operation of subtraction, the adult calls "eight minus three" and "Six minus zero."

CONCEPTS: BASIC ADDITION FACTS; BASIC SUBTRACTION
FACTS

Activity: Number Man (Variation)

Each player is assigned a number and stands behind a line at one end of the play area. One player, the Number Man, calls out addition and subtraction problems such as "Five plus six" and "Twelve minus four." The players who have the number, which is the answer (the missing sum or addend), for the problem must try to get past the Number Man to the line on the opposite side without being tagged. If tagged, the player must help the Number man. The adult will probably want to reassign numbers frequently and have players change places with the Number Man.

Application: Reinforcement is provided for recalling missing addends and sums.

CONCEPTS: ONE LESS THAN; MEANING OF SUBTRACTION

Activity: Dodge Ball

The group is divided into two teams. One team forms a circle and the other team stands inside the circle. The regular game of Dodge Ball is played, with players comprising the circle trying to hit the team members in the center with a large rubber ball such as a beach ball below the waist. The players in the center, to avoid being hit, may move about, jump, stoop, but they may not go outside the circle. When a player in the center is hit, he or she becomes a part of the circle. Each time a player is hit, the team forming the circle calls out the subtraction fact for the action, which has just taken place. For example, if there are ten players in the center and one is hit, the players call out "Ten minus one equals nine," before throwing the ball again. The team with the largest number of players remaining in the center at the end of two minutes wins the game.

Application: This activity enables children to decide what subtraction facts describe the physical situation they are experiencing. As the number of sentences in this activity are all presented orally, the adults may want to follow with an activity involving the writing of number sentences both horizontally and vertically.

CONCEPTS: MISSING ADDENDS; ADDEND PAIRS FOR A GIVEN SUM; BASIC SUBTRACTION FACTS, HIGHER DECADE FACTS

Activity: Who Am I?

At least two players should be assigned to represent each number, zero through nine. The players stand in a circle facing in and an object is placed in the center of the circle. When the leader makes statements such as "Subtract me from eleven and you have four," players assigned the number seven run to the center of the circle, the first player to pick up the center object scores a point, and the first player to get five points is the winner. From time to time, numbers should be reassigned.

Application: Children gain skill in recalling basic subtraction facts and finding missing addends. By using larger numbers, higher decade facts can be the focus of the activity.

CONCEPT: MULTIPLICATION BY TWO

Activity: Twice as Many

The players stand on a line near the end of the activity area and face the caller, who is standing at the finish line about 25 to 50 feet away. The caller gives directions such as "Take two hops. Now take twice as many." Directions are varied in number and type of movement. Each direction is followed by "Now take twice as many." The first player to reach the finish line calls out, "Twice as many," and everyone runs back to the starting line. The caller tags all those he or she can before they reach the starting line. All those tagged help the caller the next time.

Application: Children are able to apply their knowledge of multiplication facts for the factor two in a highly motivating activity. The adult may want to check each time a new direction is given to be sure the children have multiplied by two accurately and have the correct answer. Those children having difficulty could be helped to act out the multiplication fact called for.

CONCEPTS: MULTIPLES, MULTIPLICATION FACTS

Activity: Back to Back

The players stand back to back with arms interlocked at the elbows. The adult points to each group and, with the help of the children, counts by twos. If one player is left, the number one is added and total number of players is thereby determuined. If the adult calls for a group of two the players must find a new partner. Each time the players are regrouped they count by twos, threes, whatever is appropriate, and add the number of players left. (If the resulting number is not the total number of players present, there has been an error and groups should be counted again.) Whenever the number called for is larger than the group already formed, the adult may choose to ask how many players are needed for each group to become the size group that has just been called for. Whatever the size of group that is called for, the players must hook up back to back in groups of that number. A time limit may be set. The players who arc lcft may rcjoin thc group cach timc thcrc is a call to rcgroup.

Application: This activity not only provides experience with the multiples of a given factor, but also informally prepares children for uneven division. In fact, they may want to predict the number of children who will be left before the signal to start regrouping is given. If a chalkboard is available, the adult may choose to write number sentences to record each regrouping. For example, if there are 25 children and groups of four have been called for, the record should show that six fours and one is 25 or $(6 \times 4) + 1 = 25$.

CONCEPTS: MULTIPLES OF WHOLE NUMBERS; COMMON MULTIPLES

Activity: Multiple Squat

Players stand in a line or a circle, and each is assigned a number in order, starting with one. The players say their number in return. However, when their number is a multiple of three they squat but do not speak. A common variation requires that players also squat for any number for which the numeral has the digit of three in it. Multiples of different numbers can be used, of course. A more complex variation involves squatting for a multiple of either of two designated numbers; that is, three and four.

Application: Children develop skill in determining the set of multiples for a specified whole number. The activity can be adapted for more advanced children by having them squat only for common multiples of two numbers. For the numbers two and three they would squat for six, twelve, etc. children should be reassigned numbers frequently.

CONCEPTS: ONE-DIGIT FACTORS OF A WHOLE NUMBER; DIVISION WITH ONE DIGIT DIVISORS; ONE AS A FACTOR OF EVERY WHOLE NUMBER TWO AS FACTOR OF EVEN NUMBERS; RULES FOR DIVISIBILITY

Activity: Factor First

Nine players wear or hold cards with one of the numerals one through nine. They stand on the outside of a circle facing in, and an object such as a bowling pin is placed in the center of the circle. When the leader calls out a number (such as 21) all players who have a number, which is a factor of the number, called run to the center of the circle. The first player to pick up the center object gets a point. If a player whose number is not a factor should pick up the object, he or she loses two points. Play proceeds until the first player gets a predetermined number of points. It is important that numbers be assigned rather frequently and regularly. For example, cards can be passed to the person on the left after every third or fourth play.

Application: Children become proficient in finding a missing one-digit factor, a skill necessary for division computation. Some children may also note for the first time that one is a factor of every whole number, or that two is a factor of every whole number with 0, 2, 4, 6, or 8 in the units place. Rules for divisibility can be applied to larger numbers when children have studied them.

CONCEPT: MEANING OF DIVISION (MEASUREMENT)

Activity: Triplet Tag

The players form groups of three, with hands joined. After the groups are formed , the adult should write a division statement pointing out that the number of players in the group is the product, and the size of the groups is the known factor. To find the unknown factor the groups are counted. If one or two players are left over, that number is the remainder and it is also recorded. The groups stand scattered about the activity area. One group is *It* and carries a red cloth. The *It* groups try to tag another group of three. Hands must be joined at all times. When a group is tagged, it is given the red cloth, and the activity continues.

Application: In this activity, children act out measurement meaning of division. By taking a moment to record the numbers in a division statement, children can relate the situation to the symbols they will use when working with paper and pencil.

CONCEPTS: MEANING OF DIVISION (MEASUREMENT); EFFECT OF INCREASING OR DECREASING THE DIVISOR

Activity: Birds Fly South

Play begins with the entire group distributed randomly behind a starting line. The number of players in the group is the dividend (or product). A caller gives the signal to play by calling "Birds fly south in flocks of six" (or the largest divisor that will be used). The group runs to another line that has been designated as "South." At this point the group should be grouped in sixes. After observing the number of flocks (the quotient), the players who remain (that is, those who were not able to be included in one of the flocks) become hawks who take their places between the two lines. Then with the call "Scatter! The hawks are coming!" the players run back to the other line, with the hawks attempting to tag them. Note is taken of who is tagged. Play continues, with the entire group taking its place behind the starting line. The caller then uses the next lower number for the call. If six was used first, five would be called next. "Birds fly south in flocks of five." This continues until groups of two have been formed and they return to the starting line. Each time the players should observe the number of flocks that are formed. To score the activity, each player begins with a score, which is the number called first. In the case illustrated above the number would be six. If a player is tagged, his or her score decreases by a point.

Application: At the end of the activity, consider the arithmetic, which has been applied. If possible, record division number sentences showing the number of flocks formed when different divisors were used for the same dividend. Help the children form the generalization that, for a given dividend (product), when the divisor (known factor) decreases, the quotient (unknown factor) increases in value. After this pattern is established, the numbers called can be reversed beginning with the smallest divisor and working up to the highest divisor to be used. Here, the converse of the previous statement can be developed.

CONCEPTS: BASIC FACTS OF ARITHMETIC; GREATER THAN AND LESS THAN; FACTORS AND MULTIPLES; COMMON FACTORS AND GREATEST COMMON FACTOR; PRIME NUMBERS

Activity: Catch the Thief

The group is divided into two teams of equal number, and members of each team are assigned a number, starting with one for each team. Teams line up 20 or 25 feet apart, and an object is placed at the center so that it is equidistant from the two teams. As players line up it is not necessary that they line up in ordinal sequence. Whenever the leader signals, the appropriate player or players from both sides run to the center and try to pick up the object and take it across their line before being tagged by a member of the other team. When successful, one point is scored for the team. The team with the highest score wins. The choice of appropriate signals for play will depend upon previous experiences of the players. Suggestions include:

"Less than four"
"The sum of five and six"
"The difference between twelve and seven"
"Multiples of four"
"The product of three and five"
"Factors of 24"
"Common factors of eight and twelve"
"Greater than eight and less than twelve"
"Primes"
"The greatest common factor of 12 and 18"

Application: Children reinforce a number of skills, depending upon the choice of signals for play. A call such as "Multiples zero" will help children generalize the zero property for multiplication as they observe that no children run forward. Also, attention can be directed to the fact that whenever factors for a given number are called for, children with the number one and the given number always get to run. The idea of the empty set is applied with a call like "Greater than five and less three." To reinforce correct interpretation of similar symbolic (visual) expressions, and overhead projector can be used for presenting the signal.

CONCEPT: MULTIPLICATION OF FRACTIONS

Activity: Fraction Race

The group is divided into a number of teams. Members of each team take a sitting position, one behind the other a specified distance form a goal line. Starting with the first player on each team, each player is assigned a number (one, two, etc.). The adult calls out a multiplication combination including a fraction and a whole number. The players whose number is the product stand, run to the goal line, and return to their original sitting position. If the adult calls out "One-fourth times eight," all the number twos would run. Similarly, if the adult calls, "Two-thirds times twelve," all the number eights would run. The first player back scores five points for his or her team, the second player back scores three points and the last player scores one point.

Application: This activity helps children to determine the product of a fraction and a whole number quickly and accurately. Adjust the difficulty of the examples to the experience of the children.

Chapter 14

DEVELOPING OTHER MATHEMATICAL CONCEPTS THROUGH ACTIVE PLAY

In this chapter there are activities using concepts from geometries of one, two, and three dimensions. There are also activities that will facilitate instruction in measurement, and in addition, there are activities that focus on telling time and on coins and their values.

As in the two previous chapters, for each activity described, the mathematics concepts and skills involved are listed, thereby aiding the adult in finding activities which incorporate the content for which the children have the prerequisite background.

Following each description of an activity, suggested applications of the activity are discussed. For example, some activities can be used for initiating a concept and others help children visualize figures and relative values. There are activities during which children discuss and sharpen ideas. Other activities provide needed reinforcement for concepts and skill.

Many of the activities described in this chapter and in previous chapters can be varied to incorporate concepts from other areas of mathematics. An excellent example of an activity which can be adapted for uses with many mathematics topics is *Word Race*, described later in this chapter. In fact, it is possible to vary activities sufficiently that active play can be included in the instructional program for almost every topic in mathematics.

CONCEPT: ONE- AND TWO-DIMENSIONAL GEOMETRIC FIGURES

Activity: Show a Shape

Players are scattered about the activity area, far enough apart that each player has space for swinging arms and moving about. The leader calls "Take two turns and show a _____," specifying the two-dimensional geometric figure each player is to form with the arms or body. All players turn around twice, then form the figure named. For example, a circle can be suggested easily with both arms overhead as hands touch. By bending elbows but keeping hands and forearms rigid, different quadrilaterals can be formed. A player who touches his or her toes while keeping the legs straight makes a triangle. At times have players work in pairs to form figures. Lines, line segments, rays, and angles can also be shown. Players can let their extended arms represent a part of a line, with a fist used suggest an endpoint. Acute, right and obtuse angles can all be pictured in this way. It could be a good idea for the adult to go over some of these possibilities before the players engage in the activity.

Application: This activity helps children to learn that geometric figures are not just marks on paper, but that they consist of a set of locations in space. The activity can be used to introduce selected definitions such as an obtuse angle. However, because many of the figures formed will be suggestive rather than precise, the activity will usually be used for reinforcement.

CONCEPTS: TRIANGLE; POLYGONS

Activity: Triangle Run

A large triangle is marked off with a base at each vertex. Three teams of equal size are formed, and one team stands behind each base. On a signal the first player of each team leaves his or her base and runs to the right around the triangle, touching each base on the way. After returning to base, the next player on the team does the same. The runners may pass each other, but they must touch each base as they run. The first team back to its original place wins.

Application: This activity helps to demonstrate certain properties of a triangle, for example, the three angles. It is best to mark off different-shaped triangles from time to time so that the properties observed can be generalized to all triangles. Other polygons can be illustrated by forming more than three teams.

CONCEPT: RADIUS OF A CIRCLE

Activity: Jump the Shot

Eight to ten players form a circle, facing the center. One player stands in the center of the circle with a beanbag tied to the end of a rope. The center player swings the rope around in a large circle low to the surface area in order for the beanbag to pass under the feet of those in the circle. The players in the circle attempt to jump over the beanbag as it passes beneath their feet, for when the beanbag or rope touches a player, it is a point against him or her. The player with the lowest score wins at the end of a period of a minute or less. The player in the center may then exchange places with a player in the circle.

Application: The activity can be used to help children visualize the radius of a circle. They should note that the rope, which represents the radius, is the same length from the center to any point along the circle.

CONCEPTS: A CIRCLE IS A SIMPLE CLOSED CURVE; THE INTERIOR OF A CIRCLE

Activity: Run Circle Run

The group forms a circle by holding hands and facing inward. Depending on the size of the group, players count off by twos or threes (for small groups) or fours, fives or sixes (for larger groups of around 30). The adult calls one of the assigned numbers. All the players with that number start running around the circle in a specified direction. Each runner tries to tag one or more players running ahead of him or her. As a successful runner reaches his or her starting point without being tagged, he or she stops. Runners who are tagged go to the interior of the circle. Another number is called, and the same procedure is followed. Continue until all have been called, then reform the circle, assign new numbers to the players and repeat. As the number of players decreases, a smaller circle can be drawn on the surface area inside the larger circle; the players must stay out of the smaller circle when running around their places.

Application: Help the children notice that when they form a circle by holding hands, they make a continuous simple, closed shape. As they play the game, they should observe what happens to the size within the circle, the interior of the circle.

CONCEPT: INTERIOR OF A FIGURE

Activity: Three Bounce Relay

Teams are formed and make rows behind a starting line. A small circle about one foot in diameter is drawn 15 feet in front of the starting line before each team. At a signal the first player on each team runs with a ball to the circle. At the circle he or she attempts to bounce the ball three times within the circle; that is, in the interior of the circle. If the ball at any time does not land on the interior, the player must start over from the starting line. When a player has bounced the ball three times within the circle, he or she returns to the starting line and touches the next player, who does the same thing. The first team to finish wins.

Application: The word *interior* is stressed in explaining the activity. The children can thus learn the meaning of this term by practical use. However, so that children do not associate the term only with circular regions, other geometric shapes can be drawn from time to time.

CONCEPTS: GEOMETRIC FIGURES; MATHEMATICAL VOCABULARY (VARIED TOPICS)

Activity: Word Race

Two teams are selected, and both line up along a base line. Identical sets of cards are prepared for each team, with each card showing a definition or phrase in bold letters. The cards are distributed to members of the two teams with one card (or possibly two) per player. The leader stands beside a box on the surface area about 25 feet from the base line. He or she has a set of word cards with letters large enough to be read by the players. When the leader holds up a word card, the player with each team with the matching definition or phrase card runs to place the card in the box. The first team placing the correct card in the box wins a point. In order to minimize confusion as to which card is placed in the box first, different colors can be used for the two sets of cards.

Application: Children have many opportunities to discuss the definitions of mathematical terms as this activity progresses, and they learn much from each other. In fact, questions or misunderstandings may come to light which the adult will want to deal with at an appropriate moment. A few examples of words for word cards and of matching definitions or phrases are listed below, but adults will be able to think of others which relate directly to mathematics which is the immediate focus of instruction. Of course, it is necessary to use definitions appropriate to the child's level of development.

Leader's Word Card	Matching Card for Team Member
triangle	a polygon with three sides
rhombus	a polygon with four sides
interior	includes all points inside
radius	from the center to the circumference
addend	tells how many in one of two parts of a set

CONCEPTS: GEOMETRIC FIGURES; MATHEMATICAL VOCABULARY (VARIED TOPICS)

Activity: Have You Seen My Friend?

Each player is assigned a mathematical name. For example, one player may be triangle and another a cube. Players could also be assigned names like factor, zero, and centimeter. Names should be printed on cards and either pinned on each player or placed around the neck with a string. Appropriately named, the players stand or sit in a circle. One player is *It*, and he or she walks around the outside of the circle. Eventually, *It* stops behind one of the players and asks, "Have you seen my friend?" the player in the circle answers, "What is your friend like?" *It* describes the mathematical concept which is the name of one of the other players in the circle. *It* may say, "My friend is a polygon and has four sides." The player in the circle attempts to guess which other player is being described, and as soon as he or she guesses correctly that player is chased around the outside of the circle. The player being chased tries to run around the circle and return to his or her place without being tagged by the chaser. If tagged, he or she becomes *It*. If not tagged by the chaser, the chaser becomes *It*. The player who was *It* before the chase merely steps into the place made vacant by the chaser.

Application: During this activity, discussion concerning correct and adequate definitions of mathematical concepts are likely to evolve. For example, if a child describes the friend as "a polygon with four sides" and one child is named "square" and another "rhombus," the fact that the description could have applied to either is likely to come to light. When selecting mathematical terms to use, needed reinforcement can be provided by focusing on ideas which have been studied recently.

CONCEPTS: PARALLEL LINES; RIGHT ANGLES

Activity: Streets and Alleys

The players divide into three or more parallel lines with at least three feet between players in each direction. A runner and a chaser are chosen. The players all face the same direction and join hands with those on each side forming "streets" between the rows. Dropping hands, the players make a quarter turn and join hands again and form "alleys." The chaser tries to tag the runner going up and down the streets and alleys but not breaking through or going under arms. During the activity, the adult aids the runner by calling "streets" or "alleys" at the proper time. At this command the players drop hands, turn and grasp hands in the other direction, thus blocking the passage for the chaser. When caught, the runner and chaser select two others to take their places.

Application: Children should be helped to notice that the lines of children represent parallel lines. Further, when the adult calls "alleys" and the children make a quarter turn, children can associate the turn with a right angle.

CONCEPTS: CIRCLE; INSIDE AND OUTSIDE; EXPLORATION OF SPACE

Activity: Inside Out

The group is divided into teams of four or more, and players on each team join hands to form a circle in which each player is facing toward the inside. When the leader calls, "Inside out," each team tries to turn its circle inside out. That is, while continuing to hold hands the players move so as to face out instead of in. To do this, a player will have to lead his or her team under the joined hands of two team members. The first team to complete a circle with players facing toward the outside of the circle wins.

Application: This activity is designed as a kind of puzzle or problem-solving activity, for the goal is presented to the children and they are not told how it is possible to turn the circle inside out. It is designed to be the initial encounter with the process involved.

CONCEPT: THE SHORTEST DISTANCE BETWEEN TWO POINTS IS A STRAIGHT LINE

Activity: Straight-Crooked Relay

The group is divided into two or more teams. In the relay have one team run directly between two points while the second team has an additional place to tag between the two points that is not in direct line with the other points. Teams should be switched so that they alternate, having to run the crooked route. Also, if desired the teams taking the crooked route can start with a little bit of a head start.

Application: The children can notice that it takes less time to move between two points by following a straight line than by a crooked line because it is the shortest distance. The children can measure the straight and crooked lines between two points that are equidistant for the teams. To account for individual differences of children, the adult might make sure that both slow and fast runners are assigned to each team.

CONCEPTS: THE MEANING OF PERIMETER; THE SHORTEST DISTANCE BETWEEN TWO POINTS IS A STRAIGHT LINE

Activity: Around the Horn

A small playing area is set up similar to a baseball diamond with a home plate and three bases. The team in the field has a catcher on home plate and two fielders on each of the bases. The runners of the other team stand at home plate. The catcher has the ball. The object of the activity is for the catcher and fielders, upon a signal, to relay the ball around the bases and back to home plate *twice* before the runner at home plate can run around and tag each base and proceed to home plate *once*. At the bases the fielders take turns. One takes the first throw, the other the second. The team up to the plate scores a point if it reaches home plate before the ball.

Application: The distance around the bases is described as the perimeter of the field. Each runner is told he or she must run the perimeter of the field, and the team in the field is told that the ball must go twice around the perimeter of the field. The children learn that a wild throw which is not in a straight line to the other player takes longer to get to the next base.

CONCEPT: RECOGNITION OF COINS

Activity: Stepping Stones

On the activity area draw a stream with stepping stones arranged so that a player can take different paths across the stream. Place a coin on each stepping stone. Caution the players not to fall in the stream by making a mistake naming coins. As a player chooses a stepping stone to cross the stream and step on the stone, he or she must name the coin and its value. Other players watch for mistakes. A successful crossing scores one point for the player. It is important to change coins frequently.

Application: This activity provides an interesting context for children to practice naming coins and stating their value. As children watch, they too are involved in the activity, confirming and/or rejecting their own ideas about the coins.

CONCEPT: VALUES OF COINS

Activity: Bank

One player is selected to be the Bank. The rest of the players stand at a starting line about 20 feet from the Bank. Bank calls out the number of pennies, nickels, or dimes a player may take. (A penny is one small step; a nickel equals five penny steps; and a dime equals ten penny steps.) Bank calls a player's name and says, "Mary, take three pennies." Mary must answer, "May I?" Then Bank says "Yes, you may" or "No, you may not." If Mary forgets to say "May I?" she must return to the starting line. The first player to reach the Bank become the Bank. All players should be called upon.

Application: By taking steps forward toward the Bank, children gain an understanding that a nickel has the same value as five pennies and a dime has the same value as ten pennies. The adult may want to encourage each child to say before moving forward how many steps he or she is allowed to take.

CONCEPT: VALUES OF COINS

Activity: Banker and the Coins

Each player is given a sign to wear which denotes one of the following: five cents, ten cents, twenty-five cents, fifty cents, nickel, dime, quarter, or half-dollar. One player is the Banker, who call out different amounts of money up to one dollar. The players run and group themselves with other players until their total group totals the amount of money called by the Banker. Every player who is part of a correct group gets a point.

Application: Children gain practice in combining different amounts of money to arrive at a specific amount. They learn that there are usually several ways one can combine coins to produce a specified amount of money. As the adult checks that a group is correct, he or she can have the whole group count it out. In this way, children will more likely learn about values of coins if they are not sure.

CONCEPT: TELLING TIME

Activity: Tick Tock

The group forms a circle that represents a clock. Two players are runners and they are called Hour and Minute. The players chant "What time is it?" Minute then chooses the hour and calls it out (six o'clock). Hour and Minute must stand still while the players in the circle call "one o'clock, two o'clock...six o'clock (or whatever time has been chosen). When the players get to the chosen hour, the chase begins. Hour chases Minute clockwise around the outside of the circle. If Hour can catch Minute before the players in the circle once again call out "one o'clock, two o'clock, three o'clock...six o'clock (the same hour as counted the first time), he or she chooses another player to become Hour. The activity can also be played counting by half-hours.

Application: Children not only get practice in calling the hours in order but also gain experience with the concept of the term *clockwise*.

CONCEPT: LINEAR MEASUREMENT; AVERAGE (MEAN); ADDITION (INCLUDING DECIMALS)

Activity: Add-A-Jump Relay

The group is divided into teams, and each team has one player serving as a marker and one player serving as scorekeeper. Teams form rows in relay formation. The first player on each team moves up to the starting line in front of the team and jumps as far as he or she can. The team's marker indicates where the player landed, then the player who jumped measures the distance, and the second player on the team moves to the starting line and jumps. The relay continues until all team members have jumped. Scorekeepers add the measurements, and the team with the greatest total distance is the winner.

Application: In addition to developing measuring skills further, this activity provides practice in addition and experience comparing distances. Either English or metric units can be used for measuring. More advanced children could measure in meters and express the distance with a decimal including tenths and hundredths (to the nearest centimeter). The children can use the figures that were recorded to find the average distance jumped and to compare team or individual records with previously established records.

CONCEPT: LIQUID MEASUREMENT (PINTS AND QUARTS)

Activity: Milkman Tag

Two teams of three milkmen are selected and given milk truck bases. One team might be called Chocolate, and the other White. The remaining players are called Pints. On a signal one milkman from each team tries to tag one of the Pints. When he or she tags one, they both go to the milk truck, and another milkman goes after a Pint. The adult sets a goal of so many quarts to be gained in order to win. The players must then figure out how many Pints will be needed to make the necessary number of quarts.

Application: Children are provided a highly motivating activity for applying the idea of two Pints are equivalent to one quart. Children may want to group Pints in twos in order to determine how many quarts each team has.

Chapter 15

LEARNING ABOUT WRITING
THROUGH ACTIVE PLAY

Where, and by whom writing as a form of communication was first developed remains unknown. However, some scholars place the beginning of writing at 6,000 B. C.[1]

It is estimated that about 75 percent of the waking hours are spent in verbal communication, and 9 percent of this time is spent in writing as compared to 45 percent in listening, 30 percent in speaking, and 16 percent in reading. Simply because only 9 percent of the waking hours are spent expressing ourselves through writing is no reason to minimize its importance. No doubt the reason for this low percentage figure is that there are far fewer opportunities to express ourselves in writing than in speaking, in the same way that there are far fewer ways to receive the thoughts and feelings of others through reading than there are through listening. Yet, reading is considered by many to be the most important communicative skill.

Since so little attention appears to have been given to the *basic R of writing* as compared to reading and mathematics, it is important to go into some detail in this chapter about some of the concerns of writing before getting into how to help the child learn to write and improve upon this ability through active play.

Almost all children want to write, and prior to starting school many children make an attempt. The child's desire to write most likely comes from a feeling that he or she can create something by scribbling on a piece of paper and from wanting to imitate. Usually between the ages of three and four years, the young child makes marks for his or her name on birthday and Christmas cards to relatives and friends. From four to six years of age the child may try to write his or her name or copy a "thank you" note that has been dictated to a parent or older brother or sister. At an early age children have been known, much to the alarm of some parents, to write on the walls to express themselves. Unfortunately, too many children are punished for this practice when they should be rewarded by being provided with writing materials to express themselves.

For the most part, children enter first grade with a desire to write. As the child develops, and grows in ability to express thoughts and feelings well, he or she moves from writing one sentence "on his own" to writing many sentences involving length and structure and the organization of ideas into paragraphs.

It should be noted that merely providing opportunities to write will not necessarily mean that children will improve their writing. Direct guidance is needed by parents and teachers. Both parents and teacher should recognize that skills should be considered as a means to an end and not necessarily ends in themselves. The important factors to consider are that (1) most all children want to write, and (2) they will perhaps write with originality, creativity, and spontaneity.

There is a high relationship between spelling and writing. To learn to spell a word the child uses the same recognition skills that are used reading. As the child writes, he or she spells the word that he or she has heard (listening), has spoken (speaking), and has read (reading). These relationships make it easier for the child to spell.

Handwriting involves physical coordination and manipulation. Thus, among other things, handwriting involves the use of muscles and bones of the hand and wrist. In addition, it is concerned with a high-level refinement between the hands and the eyes. As far as total language development is concerned, writing is preceded by listening, speaking and reading. The child develops a listening vocabulary, and will likely try to put into oral language the words he or she hears. Next, the child may read about things that are of interest, and finally will try to put into writing those things with which he or she is familiar.

For the above reason, it is the general opinion that *manuscript* writing may be best suited for children at the primary school level. In this type of writing all the letters of the alphabet are formed with straight lines and circles or parts of circles. The size of the writing tends to decrease with the child's development. Although the research in this area is inconclusive, the trend appears to be much in favor of manuscript for the beginners. Children who begin their writing experiences with manuscript seem to write more freely. They use a larger number of different words than do most children who begin with the *cursive* form. This form (cursive) requires the joining of letters into words, and it introduces varying dergrees of slantong. It is also interesting to note that children who begin their school experiences with manuscript seem to spell a larger number of words correctly than do children who begin with cursive writing. (Later in the chapter there will be a more detailed discussion of manuscript and cursive writing.)

Learning to write is a highly individualized skill. To serve its purpose as a form of communication, legible handwriting should be produced with ease and adequate speed. An important aspect is the development of what might be called a "handwriting consciousness" or the desire to write well so that others may read it easily. Adults can be most helpful to children in this regard.

WRITING READINESS

It is necessary for adults to have some understanding of the importance of writing readiness so that they will not unwittingly push children into writing before they are ready for this experience.

As was the case with reading readiness and mathematics readiness, children need to progress through certain developmental stages as far as writing readiness is concerned. There appears to be a marked relationship between maturity and writing readiness because, among other things, writing is dependent upon skill movement, manual dexterity and eye-hand coordination. Movements of the eyes tend to develop sooner than the more refined finger movements. Therefore, the former will guide the writing hand as the child begins to write. At a later time both of these movements become coordinated to the extent that writing becomes more or less an automatic process.

An important writing readiness factor for the adult to keep in mind is that it is a common characteristic for children to reverse letters such as writing *d* for *b*. this is likely due to the limited development of eye-hand coordination previously mentioned, and it can be expected to occur in children at five or six years of age. In fact, immature development in eye-hand coordination may continue in some children until they are well beyond six years of age.

Alert teachers are sensitive to the importance of writing readiness, and ordinarily they will tend to spend some time on readiness skills at the outset of the writing program when a child enters school.

MANUSCRIPT AND CURSIVE WRITING

I have already mentioned the difference between manuscript and cursive writing. In manuscript writing the letters are formed by straight lines and circles or parts of circles, while cursive writing requires joined letters and the slanting of letters as well. This is an example of manuscript writing:

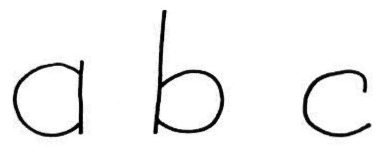

This is an example of cursive writing:

There has long been a controversy regarding these two forms of writing. Most of this has centered around when to make the transition from manuscript to cursive for the average child. At one time it was thought that children might begin cursive writing at about fourth grade. At the present time it is a more common practice to start cursive writing near the end of second grade or the beginning of third. In some instances it is felt that manuscript writing can be eliminated altogether, and that the child should start the writing experience with cursive writing. This school of thought has become more and more pronounced among those people who deal with children with learning disabilities.

In any case, the present consensus of opinion appears to be that the average child should start with manuscript writing and then proceed to cursive writing at the proper time. This means that individual difference should be taken into account and that individual children might well be permitted to develop their own style rather than being held to any given standard.

TEACHING WRITING IN SCHOOLS

If an adult is to meet with any degree of success in his or her efforts to prepare a child for school in the area of handwriting, it is important to have some idea of writing programs in schools.

It should be recognized that there is a great variation in the educational preparation of teachers as far as the teaching of handwriting is concerned. It is possible that some teachers will have had some extensive previous educational experience in the teaching of handwriting. However, it is perhaps more likely that this will not necessarily be the case. It is entirely possible that the educational experience of some may have been limited to that which was included in a course encompassing all of the areas of language development – listening, speaking, reading and writing. These statements should not be interpreted as an indictment against any of our teacher education institutions. It is simply that in most instances a great deal more time is directed to methods of teaching reading than to listening, speaking and writing combined.

Although there is some variation from one school to another, the following information suggests generally what a majority of elementary schools are attempting to do in the area of handwriting.

Several years ago the Commission of the English Curriculum of the National Council of Teachers of English proposed four objectives of writing. The first of these was *ease* in writing. If a child can approach the task with confidence and a sense of adequacy he or she can put energy into making writing serve his or her purpose and often find pleasure in doing it. The second objective was *clarity*, which is intimately associated with ease. The third objective, *suitability* in writing, is highly important for all social purposes, and the fourth objective, *originality* adds flavor and interest for both writer and reader. In general, most elementary schools appear to be trying to reach these goals in the curriculum area of writing.

As in all school subjects, the teaching of handwriting proceeds from the less difficult to the more difficult tasks. The usual sequence of events involves *readiness skills, manuscript writing,* and *cursive writing.* To provide for orderly, achievement of the child in handwriting, these tasks are divided in the specific skills required for each task.

Readiness Skills

Readiness skills are mainly concerned with the writing *strokes* that will eventually be used to form manuscript letters. These strokes are ordinarily taught in the following sequence:

1. Vertical lines. (The stroke is from the top to the bottom.)

2. Horizontal lines. (The stroke is from the left to right.)

3. Backward circle. (The stroke starts at the beginning of the arrow.)

4. Up and over half circle. (The stroke goes up and then down.)

5. Down and under half circle. (The stroke goes down and then up.)

6. Forward circle. (The stroke starts at the beginning of the arrow.)

7. Right slanting line. (The stroke starts at the top and slants to the right.)

8. Left slanting line. (The stroke starts at the top and slants to the left.)

An adult may wish to try some of these readiness strokes with the preschool child. Before asking the child to apply the strokes on paper with a crayon or large pencil, it can be useful to have the child make large strokes in the air. This can serve the purpose of having the child "get the feel" of the movement before making direct application of it with paper and pencil.

Manuscript Writing

In general, when children begin manuscript writing, paper with ruled lines is used. The reason for using lined paper is that it makes it easier for the child to form letters. It provides the child with an opportunity to judge height relationships of letters to each other as well as the available writing space.

Some persons feel that it may be wise to begin the writing experience with unlined paper. The main reason given for this practice is that it provides the child with a more relaxed and rhythmic pattern of writing. For example, the lower case (small letter) of *l* is simply a vertical stroke line, while the upper case (capital letter) of *L* is a vertical and horizontal stroke. This can be done easily without the use of lined paper.

A widely used handwriting program, which has been developed by the Zaner-Bloser Company of Columbus, Ohio, recommends the following manuscript writing sequence for children.

l L, i I, t T
o O, c C, a A, e E
r R, m M, n N, u U, s S
d D, f F, h H, b B
v V, w W, k K, x X, z Z
g G, y Y, p P, j J, q Q

Adults who would like to assist preschool children with handwriting might want to consider this sequence rather than having the child use traditional alphabetical order.

Cursive Writing

As previously mentioned, cursive writing differs from manuscript writing because it involves more of a slant, and the letters are joined together to form a word. After the child has become reasonably proficient in manuscript writing, under skillful guidance he or she makes the transition from manuscript to cursive writing.

Usually, the child is afforded the opportunity to view both manuscript and cursive writing to see some of the similarities and differences. Many classrooms have permanent examples of both manuscript and cursive writing on the chalkboard, and this is helpful to the child. Ordinarily, the teacher will demonstrate the slanting and joining of letters on the chalkboard to show the movement from manuscript to cursive writing. Teachers who deal with children in this stage of their writing development report that there is a great deal of eagerness on the part of the children to get into cursive writing.

Handedness

Handedness of the child is not necessarily a problem if it is detected early. If the adult is reasonably sure that the child has established a preference for the left hand before entering school, this information should be given to the teacher. Teachers themselves can identify preferred handedness by observing the hand used in certain activities.

The main factor taken into account for left-handed children is that of position. When using the chalkboard the child can stand at the left side and when seated he or she should also be on the left side. The purpose of this is to keep a left-handed child and a right-handed child from interfering with each other as they proceed with their handwriting experience.

SOME GUIDELINES FOR ADULTS IN HELPING CHILDREN WITH WRITING

Any assistance the adult gives the child in handwriting *after* he or she enters school should perhaps be done in close cooperation with the child's teacher. However, much can be done by the adult to assist the preschool child with the handwriting experience. As in any teaching situation, the adult is not expected to be an expert. Nevertheless, it is hoped that the reader might be able to make application of some of the suggestions submitted in this section of the chapter, both for the benefit of the preschool child as well as the child who has already started school. Before getting into some specific guidelines for adults, I would like to give some consideration to what is known about the handwriting of children before they enter school.

As I have stated before, learning to read and learning to write are processes that are concerned with verbal symbols. In reading, the reader *receives* information by trying to extract meaning from symbols, and in writing, the writer *expresses* meaning by applying the symbols with the use of combined eye-hand movements.

Although the usual sequence of language development is considered to be listening, speaking, reading, and writing, there is evidence that suggests that some children write before formal instruction, and in some cases they write before they read. In fact, some investigators have found that writing can begin as early as three and one-half years of age, with the most prevalent time for the child's *interest* in writing beginning at age four. There are even some researchers who suggest that the teaching of handwriting precede the teaching of reading. This is based on the idea that the formation of letters, either using sets of letters or writing by hand, is the first step toward reading. It should be mentioned again, however, that the prevailing recommendation for language development still favors the sequence of listening, speaking, reading, and writing.

It has been clearly demonstrated that a *home reading environment* can have a very positive influence on the reading interest and ability of the child when he or she enters school. However, there has not been a great deal of investigation done with regard to the *home writing environment.* Nevertheless, there appears to be certain factors in the home environment that are useful in improving the child's interest and ability in writing before starting school.

With the above comments serving as a background of information, the following guidelines are submitted for the reader's consideration.

1. There are many different ways that a child holds a pencil. The general recommendation is that the child should hold it with the index finger and thumb, with the pencil resting on the middle finger and where the index finger and thumb meet. This position makes the pencil an extension of the forearm. If the child cannot hold the pencil in position, it may mean that he or she has not yet developed sufficient small muscle control. This control, which begins in the larger back and shoulder muscles, can be improved by encouraging the child to do things to improve such development. Such popular activities as swinging and climbing are important to such development.
2. Proper placement of writing paper is very important. The child can sit in a chair with the back straight. The next step is to have the child interlock fingers, folding the hands on the table. The joined hands form a triangle with the front part of the upper body. The paper is then placed under the writing hand. For right-handed children the head is turned slightly to the left, with the opposite position for left-handed children.
3. If the child is left-handed there might be a slight variation from the right-handed child in the use of paper and pencil. The child may need to turn the paper slightly to the left, and hold the pencil in such a way that he or she can see the writing. It should be recognized that for a

left-handed child, right to left is a more natural movement. The child can be told that he or she always starts to write on the same side of the paper as that of the writing hand. (I have already mentioned the importance of placement when both left- and right-handed children are involved.)

4. A child may have difficulty making strokes from top to bottom (as shown in the section on writing readiness skills). If this is the case, it may be helpful with some children to have them practice swinging their arms from front to back and from side to side. The purpose of this is to help the child develop a feeling of rhythmic movement.

5. Practically all children enjoy finger painting, and this experience can be helpful to the child in the beginning-to-write activities. With the finger painting process the child can get the feel of letter formations by making circles, parts of circles, and lines. After this experience the same can be tried with a pencil.

6. With some children, when they are beginning to form letters, it is a good practice to associate the letter with something to arouse the child's interest. For example, an *O* is like an orange, or an *S* is like a worm.

7. A practice called "talk writing" can be used with success. This involves having the child "say" the action as the letter is formed. For example, in forming the upper case *L*, you could have the child say "down" when making the vertical stroke downward and "across" when making the horizontal stroke.

8. You can make a part of a letter and then have the child complete it. You can also have the child make part of a letter and you can complete it.

9. If there is a typewriter in the home, allow the child to experiment with it. This experience can be very enjoyable for the child, and it can be help with small muscle control problems if they exist.

ACTIVE PLAY EXPERIENCES INVOLVING WRITING

Since handwriting is more or less restricted to a combination of fine muscle manipulations and eye movements, there are not as many opportunities for active play experiences in writing as there are in reading and mathematics.

However, those possibilities which are available through active play are very effective.

Writing about Active Play Experiences

One of the most important factors in the beginning writing experiences of children is that these experiences involve functional situations. There is wholehearted agreement among experts on the subject that emphasis should be placed upon the using of writing in daily living in relation to the real interests and concerns of children. Probably without exception, educators are subscribing to the idea that the child's ability to express himself or herself well in writing grows with the development of interests and the concerns that he or she is eager to express.

In view of modern procedures that emphasize written expression as very important in the child's school experience, it becomes essential that opportunities be provided for children to write in purposeful and meaningful situations. Certainly, one of the most meaningful experiences for the child (perhaps the *most meaningful*) is that which is derived from active play.

One of the ways that an adult can help the child to write about an active play experience is to use any of the activities appearing in the preceding chapters. The first step is to have the child tell about the activity after having engaged in it. This is known as *dictating* the experience. The child's comments are dictated to the adult who, in turn, records them on a large sheet of paper or piece of cardboard. The child observes as this is being done. The adult then goes through the child's "message" with him or her, and they read it aloud together. The next step is to have the child write about the experience by copying what the adult has recorded. This provides a great deal of motivation for the child to write because he or she is able to express in writing the enjoyable experience in which he or she engaged.

Another approach in writing about active play experiences is using the prepared stories in previous chapters. In addition to having the child try to read the story after having engaged in the activity depicted in the story, he or she can be asked to copy the story as well.

I have conducted many experiments with the above procedures. It has been found that when children engage in this type of writing activity the formation of letters (legibility) is much better than when they are asked to form letters into words under other conditions.

Body Letters

To form a letter it is important that the child develop a memory of the shape of the letter. Using the body or some of its parts to form letters can improve upon *visualization*. Previously I described this term as involving visual image, which is the mental reconstruction of a visual experience, or the result of mentally combining a number of visual experiences.

There are many ways that body letters can be formed. For example, the letter *c* can be formed with the child in a sitting position on the floor. The child bends forward at the waist, bows the head, and stretches the arms forward. The letter *c* can also be formed with body parts. The index finger and thumb can be curled to make a *c* or both arms can be used for a *c* by simply holding the arms to the side and bending them at the elbows.

The creative adult in collaboration with the child will be able to work out numerous other body letter possibilities. It is a good practice to have both the child and the adult form a body letter and then have the other guess what the letter is.

Big Pencil

When a child begins to form letters he or she should be provided the opportunity to do this in several ways. One way is for the child to pretend that he or she is a *big pencil*. The child becomes a big pencil first by standing with the hands joined in front. Next the child bends forward with arms straight and joined hands pointing toward the floor.

The adult calls out a letter and/or shows the child a large letter written in manuscript. The child goes through the movement of forming the letter by moving his or her joined hands as if he or she were a pencil.

Action Word Writing

For action word writing the adult will need to prepare materials as follows. Cut heavy cardboard (white tag board is preferred) into several pieces about 6 inches wide and 12 inches long. Such action words as *jump, hop,* and *run* are written in manuscript on one side of the card. The cards are placed in a pile a given distance away from the child. The child selects one card, does what it says, and returns to the original position. For example, if it says "jump," he or she takes several jumps back to where he or she started. When the child returns, he or she copies the word on a piece of paper and returns for another card. If desired, the activity can be timed to see how much the child improves each time the activity is played.

In closing this final chapter I would like to emphasize again that the active play medium of learning has been thoroughly tested and has proved very satisfactory as a most desirable way of learning for young children. Many active play activities have been provided, and creative adults will no doubt be able to make up others to use to help children learn.

Not only does this approach provide excellent opportunities for children to learn and improve their abilities in the 3Rs, but at the same time very enjoyable adult-child relationships can be expected to be forthcoming. The whole idea of this procedure may have been summarized best by Prince Otto von Bismarck in the 19th century when he commented that *You can do anything with children if you only play with them.*

NOTE

---

[1] The Columbia Encyclopedia, Sixth Edition, New York, *Columbia University Press*, 2000, p. 3114.

INDEX